To Bob —

May you continue
to give your excellent
to your patients and your
profession !!

[signature]

PERSONAL EXCELLENCE

PERSONAL EXCELLENCE

A System for Making Things Happen in Your Life and Your Career

By Jack Messenger

Executive Press
High Point, North Carolina

Library of Congress Catalog Card Number: 89–85531

ISBN 0–939975–04–1

Published by Executive Press
806 Westchester Drive
High Point, NC   27262

Printed in the United States of America
10 9 8 7 6 5 4 3 2

To my parents, Jack and Grace, for giving me life. They told me I would do important things in life and that I would be a leader. I hope they are proud.

Acknowledgements

My wife, Patricia, for her love and encouragement during the challenging times.

Fred and Eddie MacGee for their guidance and encouragement as
mentors and as sponsors of Dale Carnegie Training.

Elizabeth Rodda, my Dale Carnegie Course instructor.

Nido Qubein and the Staff at Creative Services, Inc. for their assistance
and guidance for this book.

The national Speakers Association for the friendship, education, and
colleagueship.

Foreword

Here is a book of brilliantly written observations about the make-up of the human success story

Jack Messenger's is the voice of a man who has devoted many years of intense research into the emotional, mental and physiological make-up of success. Everyone who reads his work, regardless of age or occupation, will extract a great amount of guidance which will enable them to achieve various levels of success.

The scope of "Personal Excellence: A System for Making Things Happen In Your Life and Career" is unusual. It deals with major things like taking responsibility for your life and maintaining a positive attitude, to the more mundane, such as appearance and time management. Yet, it treats every subject with the enthusiasm born from experience.

"Personal Excellence" should be mandatory reading for all businesses as well as all students at the high school and college level. It should be a part of all new employee orientation packages, as well as mandatory summer reading for students.

Because the ideas expressed here deal not only with success in business but with personal success in life in general, the reader who adheres to these principles will reap great benefits.

FRANK L. BOWERSOX
Chief Operating Officer
r.e. Scott mortgage co.

Contents

Overview

For years, America was positioned at the "top of the heap" in terms of economic strength. How did this young country achieve such status in less than 200 years? It happened through the efforts of hard-working people who took responsibility for their success.

It started with the pioneers—brave souls who left their home countries to adopt a new one. They took responsibility for their success because they had no alternative. Upon arriving here, they found no available products or services. Only wilderness. If they were to survive, it was up to them. Food had to be grown or hunted. They had to build their own homes, cut their own firewood and make their own clothes. Unless they were willing to do without—which likely could have proven unhealthy, if not fatal during harsh winters—the responsibility for obtaining these items fell squarely on the newcomer's shoulders.

And, don't forget, they also had to provide their own entertainment. There were no televisions, radios or motion pictures in those days, nor were there skating rinks, ball games, circuses or carnivals. In addition to being self-sufficient for all their necessities, the responsibility to entertain themselves—to make their lives enjoyable—also fell upon the pilgrim's shoulders.

Pioneers were strong people, because they had to be. Those who weren't strong didn't survive.

AMERICA BUILDS MUSCLE

Pioneers were America's first entrepreneurs. Armed only with tools, they created their homes from timber and obtained their meals from the land. In time, settlements developed, and people realized it was more lucrative to go into business for themselves by serving others. Some people opened various supply stores. Others learned trades, and customers bartered for services. Of course, as the population grew, towns and cities developed. Eventually, the uncivilized West beckoned to Easterners with an entrepreneurial spirit and a sense of adventure. Those who answered the call played by more or less the same rules as the original pioneers: if they wanted to survive, the responsibility fell upon their shoulders.

During the last half of the 19th century, America experienced the transformation from a rural-agricultural nation to an urban-industrialized society. Along with this massive change of geo-economics came the change of cultural values as well. Americans were no longer the rugged, self-reliant individualists of the pioneer age. They had become dependent on a social welfare state.

AMERICA ATROPHIES

Now we're at the final stages of the 20th century. We should be stronger than ever. Yet, we're not. The quality of this country's products and services has slipped over the years. American industry had gotten away with shoddy products for years because of a lack of competition. But since World War II, Japan has raised itself from its ruins to become one of the top manufacturing forces in the world. Other foreign importers also are giving us a run for our money. Add to that the fact that Americans just aren't as productive as they once were.

People are responsible for production. But unlike the pioneers, today's people don't seem as conscientious or as dedicated as were their forefathers. Perhaps one reason is because they don't have to be as dedicated. With so many social agencies in existence, no one is going to starve to death during a cold winter. Jobs are plentiful, and people can hold onto them by putting forth only minimal effort. With a steady income, today's Americans tend to relax more often than could their ancestors.

With circumstances comfortable by comparison, many of today's Americans lack the motivating desire to excel. With survival more or less assured, we often don't stretch to reach new heights. When anatomical muscles aren't used, they atrophy. The same is true for emotional muscle. The person who doesn't take a risk to achieve something significant probably will never achieve anything significant. And life is just too short to let that happen.

FAULTY CONCEPTS

I don't think Americans have become inherently lazy. Far from it. There are too many joggers on streets, too many weight-lifters in gyms, and too many people working excessive hours or multiple jobs for me to be convinced that most people are lazy.

Instead, I believe that most Americans have been misled by well-meaning people. Our society discourages us from taking risks, because, unlike the pioneer era, risk is no longer essential for survival. We don't reach for the brass ring because we might fall off the carousel and get hurt. But if we don't take risks, our situations won't improve. And, unfortunately, most people aren't completely satisfied with their personal situations.

Like the pioneers, however, we can still do something about our situations. Life is not a stagnant enterprise. For life to be truly enjoyable and fulfilling, growth must be seen as a long-term process—

one that ends only with life itself. If we don't act in our best interests, our best interests won't be served.

Some people believe there is only one correct answer or solution to a problem. They live their lives based on the way they think things should be, instead of the way things actually are. As a result, their lives often prove to be unfulfilling, because they've operated under faulty concepts.

I saw this clearly when I taught high school. Students seemed to be motivated by an attitude of "I must fit in." So they focused on the clothing, jargon and activities that "fit" the teen-aged subculture. Of course, this phenomenon was not restricted to this particular high school. Studies show that appearance is the main factor of teen self-esteem. Drugs, alcohol and even suicide have become viable options to more individualistic forms of self-expression.

As a result, the "message" the teens were sending was almost "anti-adult." They were on the verge of taking their places in society without the faintest idea of the basic success principles that can benefit anyone in life. So I started teaching a program called "Success With Mess." It was very well received and became a course favorite among students, many of whom told me that it literally changed the directions of their lives.

I was glad I could make a difference with those students. But, in time, I realized I could make a difference with adults who had never discovered the principles. It's never too late to trade an unsatisfying, unfulfilling way of life for a better way. And, if that's what you'd like to do, I truly believe this book can help you accomplish your goal.

WHAT YOU DON'T KNOW CAN HOLD YOU BACK

There are three levels of awareness—the things we know, the things we don't know but can learn and the things we don't know that we don't know. And when it comes to life, what we don't know can hurt us—or at least stunt our growth.

This book can help with the second and third levels of awareness—things you know you don't know and even those you don't know that you don't know. The book is divided into three sections.

The first is devoted to individual growth lifestyle. It explores how crucial taking responsibility is to our development and how vital a healthy self-image and a positive attitude is to success. From there, it points out the necessity of determining your ambitions, the benefits of good time management and the significance of selecting inspiring role models.

Section two discusses the power of personal appearance. Although appearance has no direct bearing on our skills and abilities, it often makes or breaks us in the eyes of others. If we don't make a favorable first impression, we might not get a second meeting with a potential customer or client. This section includes advice on how to present yourself in the most favorable light in terms of general appearance, clothing, posture, health and manners. All of these factors play strong roles in making a first impression.

Section three deals with professional competence. Although we must be good at what we do to succeed, we also must be able to get along with others, and a chapter on effective interpersonal interaction is included. Also, success calls for leadership qualities, and another chapter is devoted to acquainting you with those. The penultimate chapter of the book deals with creativity and offers advice on how to cultivate it—a quality that's important for virtually any job. And the final chapter addresses dealing with crises, and all of us have our share of those.

Stated simply, this book can help you succeed in any endeavor you would undertake. Let me offer you some suggestions on how you can get the most from this book.

(1) Read it several times—one for general content and once for more specific concentration.

(2) Read it as though you were having a personal conversation with me, and I am attempting to counsel you on your life

(3) Have an open mind. Be at least open to all of the possibilities made available by each suggestion. Try the suggestions on for size. If they do not fit or work, you can always go back to your way.

(4) Observe the "aha phenomenon." We read and we gain insights or "aha's" from our own creative mechanisms. Keep paper and pencil handy to record your insights.

(5) Be prepared to act. Nothing can come from new ideas unless they are acted upon or utilized. Take one idea at a time and work it until you can make an informed decision regarding the validity of it.

(6) Use the "My Personal Action Plan" section at the end of each chapter to internalize what you've read and make definite plans to use it for personal and professional growth.

(7) If for no other reason, enjoy this book as one man's attempt to challenge you to get the best out of your life and reap what it has to offer.

By following these suggestions and the principles in this book, you can increase your odds of being successful. And if that's why you bought this book, then you made the right choice. I've followed these principles, and I can attest that they've worked in my own life. They helped make me successful as a school teacher, and they've now made me successful as a professional speaker and consultant.

Acquaint yourself with them, take them to heart, and they'll work for you. Because by following them, you can become the best you are.

Section I

INDIVIDUAL GROWTH LIFESTYLE

Chapter One

Taking Responsibility

Immediately after we are born, we are scrubbed clean, carefully checked over and wrapped in a nice soft diaper. But, soon after, it seems we are fitted for straitjackets.

Of course, I'm not talking about real straitjackets—those designed to restrain people who have lost touch with reality and are restrained for their own safety and the safety of others. These straitjackets strap their arms to their torsos. I'm talking about another kind of straitjacket—not the kind you can see or touch, but a type that is powerfully restraining all the same.

These "straitjackets" are usually found on responsible people. But instead of preventing them from harming themselves, they actually prevent them from helping themselves. If worn long enough, these straitjackets can ruin people by limiting their effectiveness and stifling their personal growth.

These straitjackets are "mindsets," or a collection of beliefs that most often are imposed on us by key members of our environment.

We are born into cultural modes of behavior. On a superficial level, we are governed by laws. In our society, we are not free to commit murder, rob banks, burn buildings, drive while intoxicated or defraud the IRS without standing for the consequences if caught. Compliance with laws is part of the price responsible people pay to live in a free society.

The mindsets I'm talking about run much deeper than formal laws. They consist of customs and traditions. Our homes, schools, churches and synagogues, workplaces and society in general are filled with authority figures who tell us what to do and when to do it. Their directives often are based on tradition. And don't get me wrong: there is nothing bad about tradition—provided that a better alternative isn't available. But when there is a better choice, people who cling to customs are short-changing themselves and all who are affected by their actions.

Following tradition for tradition's sake generally offers a structure too confining for effective performance. Tradition often points out "one right way" to operate. As a result, it makes no concessions for our uniqueness as human beings. And even when tradition is believed to be the most effective practice, insistence on following it strongly discourages individuals from creating new and possibly more effective alternatives. After all, virtually all advancements and improvements in society were brought about by people who were eager and willing to break tradition. Civil rights, space travel, social protest and a host of modern inventions are realities because there were people who were dissatisfied with tradition.

TRADITION DOESN'T BREAK EASILY

But departing from tradition can be tough. When loyalty to tradition is blind, people act out of habit, and habits can be extremely difficult to break. For example, there's a story about two newlyweds.

Taking Responsibility

On their first night together after their honeymoon, the husband watched his wife prepare dinner by slicing off all four sides of a ham. The man asked his wife why she hacked up the ham, to which the woman replied, "I don't know. My mother always did it this way." Intrigued, the man telephoned his mother-in-law and posed the question to her. "I don't know," she replied. "My mother always did it this way." So, on the next visit to his wife's grandmother, the husband asked the elderly lady why she lopped off the sides of a ham before baking it.

"My pan is too small to hold the entire ham," the grandmother said.

The point is simple. Many times, we do things for tradition's sake. Either it's the way a task always has been done, or the method has been passed down through the generations for so long that we accept it without question. We totally disregard the "why's." And when tradition is the best reason for a chosen action, we are effectively wearing a straitjacket that restrains our minds.

Let me cite a personal example of how "straitjacket thinking" can inhibit an individual. I am the son of a man who was born in the mid-1920's, was reared during the Great Depression and matured during the 1940's, when America's work ethic was at its peak. The concept of that era was to graduate from high school, get a job, work for 30 to 40 years, then retire with a gold watch. That was the concept of my father's generation, and I, naturally, tried to adopt that philosophy when I became a school teacher and coach. But I eventually found that outlook was an uncomfortable restraint. I felt stagnant, uncomfortable and unfulfilled, but I didn't know why. This is not to say there is anything at all wrong with being a teacher; I just wanted something else out of life. I was becoming open to other possibilities. It was my burning desire to be a public speaker that forced me to rip out of that confining straitjacket.

I can't help but feel that many of those years were wasted, although I realize they were integral to my development. Still, I wish I had shed that straitjacket long ago. But I learned that when a person is willing to explode a patterned, inflexible personal outlook, he or she will be amazed at the possibilities that can develop. Personally, I look at life now as a canvas and a palette of paints that a person receives upon birth. And it's up to the individual to paint the portrait he or she desires.

Of course, it takes years for an artist to master the art of painting. Likewise, it often takes years for people to mature and determine what is really important to them. Like artists, all people require experience to improve. To gain experience, the artist must be willing to commit efforts to canvas and must chance ridicule and rejection when the painting is displayed. That's the risk that goes with being an artist. Likewise, people won't develop their full potential until they "paint their portraits," even though they, too, will hazard ridicule and rejection. Like it or not, a good life results from risk, and people who aren't willing to take risks wear straitjackets that will curb their development.

LIFE IS RISKY BUSINESS

Risk is a prerequisite for gain. Without risk, there is nothing. The chance of injury, damage or loss is always a possibility when seeking any kind of success. Whether people seek more muscle, money or meaningful relationships, they must expose themselves to some type of risk.

Consider the various gambles we face in life. We risk being hurt when we make friends, because friends can disappoint us. When we marry, we run the risk of eventually standing before a divorce court judge. Judging by statistics in some states, the odds that this will happen run about 50–50. Even becoming a parent involves risk. There is no law that says children must grow up to be responsible, productive adults. The person who chooses to become a parent runs the risk of personal disappointment.

Investors risk their money. Inventors risk their time and effort.

6

Neither are certain their risks will be rewarded. Physicians face the constant risk of being sued for malpractice. Successful attorneys take on cases at the risk of losing them—and their reputations. Members of the news media routinely risk slander and libel suits. Actors and writers run the risk of getting bad reviews that can adversely affect their careers.

Growth involves risk. Whenever we aspire to grow, we risk our beliefs and the long-held concepts on which we're accustomed to basing life decisions. And that's good, because some of these beliefs can inhibit our growth.

WE'RE TRAINED TO AVOID RISK

In America—the land of opportunity, where hardworking industrious individuals can go from rags to riches within a fraction of a lifetime—people often act as if they've been sentenced to a life of mediocrity. Why? They live their lives without risk, often because they've been trained to avoid it. As someone once said, "We tiptoe quietly through life hoping we can make it to death."

It begins when we're young. As children, we're taught to avoid risk on the playground to evade injury. We learn to avoid risk in the classroom to prevent appearing stupid. We avoid building new relationships to shy away from the risk of being rejected. And on and on it goes.

The following anonymous poem expresses it well:

> To laugh is to risk appearing the fool.
> To weep is to risk appearing sentimental.
> To reach out for another is to risk rejection.
> To expose feelings is to risk involvement.
> To place your ideas, your dreams, before the crowd is to
> risk loss.

To love is to risk not being loved in return.
To live is to risk dying.
To hope is to risk despair.
To try at all is to risk failure.
But—to risk we must,
because the greatest hazard in life is to risk nothing.
The man, the woman, who risks nothing,
does nothing,
has nothing,
is nothing.

We're conditioned not to take risks. So we avoid failure by avoiding success. As a result, we're conditioned to fear success, because the person who would be successful runs the risk of failing. I ask the question, "What would we do if we *knew* we couldn't fail?" As children, we lived like this. If we fell, we cried, but we got up and went at it again. As we aged, we "learned" about failure. Are we born to achieve and conditioned to fail?!

WE CHOOSE OUR LIVES

No matter what you believe, you always have been and always will be the product of your choices. If these choices are based on careful consideration of all of your possibilities, chances are you'll benefit. If they're not, you probably won't. When choices are based on traditional concepts which dictate that risk is bad and failure is shameful, we choose to act in ways to avoid risk and failure. And if we avoid risk and failure, we simultaneously avoid success. We adopt mediocre lifestyles, and we become mediocre people.

Mediocrity is what life is all about for some people. But it doesn't have to be that way. Because if boring, complacent lifestyles are the result of our choices, then fulfilling, exciting lifestyles can just as easily be ours. It's all a matter of what choices we're willing to make.

And make no mistake, the choice is ours. This book is about growth and making growth decisions. It's about taking responsibility for failure and success.

YOU CAN'T BECOME INDEPENDENT BY ABDICATING RESPONSIBILITY

Too often, children relinquish responsibility for their lives because their parents enable them to do so. Parents clean up after children because it's easier than teaching, encouraging and coaching responsibility. As a result, the children become accustomed to having someone take responsibility for them. If parents are too willing to assume the responsibility for their children's behavior, their children will be the losers. They will never develop dependability because they'll never be in a position to develop it.

Responsibility isn't promised. Unlike puberty, it doesn't automatically develop with adolescence, or even adulthood. Responsibility must be cultivated. People must subject themselves to responsibility to become responsible, much like bodybuilders subject themselves to weight-lifting exercises to build muscle. When people are deprived of opportunities to develop responsibility—either by themselves or by others—they don't develop it.

Unfortunately, people allowed to refuse responsibility for their actions often begin a habit that will follow them all of their lives. Children might think it amusing to watch others take responsibility for their actions. But the transition to adulthood signifies the acceptance of independence—a responsibility in itself that's too heavy to shoulder for people unaccustomed to assuming dependability. This is no different in the business world. Clients of mine continually complain of "dependent" employees who will not make decisions.

Irresponsible people cope with their inability to assume responsibility by blaming others for their failings.

And judging by the news media, it almost appears fashionable to point fingers for personal failings. Let me offer a few examples reported in the newspapers to prove my point:

> An Oklahoma City woman sought $147 million in damages from the U.S. Tobacco Co. because her son, who had used snuff for six years, died from cancer of the mouth.
>
> Philadelphia Flyers goalie Pelle Lindbergh died when his speeding Porsche 930 Turbo crashed into a concrete wall.
>
> According to news reports, his blood-alcohol level was .17, or the equivalent of drinking more than 11 ounces of whiskey within an hour. Yet, Lindbergh's parents and fiance claim that responsibility rests with two New Jersey bars they sued on the grounds that "they caused Pelle's death by serving him drinks when he was already visibly drunk."
>
> A man who reportedly killed nine children and two women was acquitted of manslaughter in a New York court because the jury—following the judge's interpretation of state law— found that being a cocaine addict served as "a reasonable explanation or excuse" for the 11 homicides.

These stories are true. And at the rate these "I'm-not-responsible" accounts crop up in the media, I'm expecting to see next where a killer goes scot free with the defense, "I didn't kill the police officer. My gun did it."

What's wrong with us as a society? No one twisted the young man's arm every day for six years, forcing him to dip snuff. No one placed a gun to the young hockey player's head, coercing him to drink irresponsibly. And if word gets out in New York that state law gives cocaine addicts a break, life for many "Big Apple" residents is going to get one heckuva lot rougher. It seems as though as long as you can come up with a good enough reason for an action taken, the action become acceptable *but* therefore relinquishes our control or responsibility.

WE'RE RESPONSIBLE ADULTS, NOT VICTIMS

Blaming other people and circumstances for life situations creates a "victim mentality" that actually promotes personal irresponsibility, which flourishes at the expense of our potential ability and creativity. And this very mentality is manifesting itself on a national level. American industry is foundering because foreign importers play by different rules. A high-ranking military official suggests he didn't obey the constitution because he was defending his country. Our nation is head-over-heels in debt because its leaders of recent memory haven't assumed the responsibility to balance a budget.

People who abdicate responsibility have a reason for their every failure. "I got fired because my boss doesn't understand me." "I flunked this course because my instructor didn't make learning interesting for me." "I can't make friends because my nose is too big and my ears stick out." "I can't get ahead because I'm White, Black, Hispanic, Jewish, a man, a woman." The "reasons" go on and on and on . . .

How about American savings habits? It has been said that the average 65-year-old retiree has less than $250 in a savings account. Let's look at one reason why this might be true.

Percentages Of Income Applied To Savings

	U.S.	Japan
1975	8.8%	22.1%
1980	6.2%	19.2%
1985	4.8%	17.8%

With these statistics in mind, is it a wonder that only 3% of the American population is self-sufficient at retirement? It's because most of the other 97% never accepted the responsibility to provide for their post-employment life.

WILL YOU SLIDE OR FLY?

Let's take a look at two of God's creatures—the oyster and the eagle. Immediately after birth, the oyster is set for life. It lives in its own shell, which protects it from predators. When it desires food, it has but to open its shell and filter the nourishment contained in sea water. The eagle, on the other hand, operates under a different set of circumstances. It must work for all it obtains. It must build its own nest and endure snow, ice, wind and rain to find food.

But there's another side to this story. The oyster has to pay dearly for its security. It's protective shell is also its prison, for it cannot venture out of it. Oysters also have no means of defense. This fact makes oysters easy prey for people who take grand delight in cracking open their shells, splashing them with a shot of Tabasco and letting them slide—alive and helpless—down their throats. (Remember how the late actor Robert Shaw screamed when he suffered a similar fate from the title character of the 1974 motion picture "Jaws"?)

Sure, an oyster has it easy. But who wants to be an oyster?

How about the eagle? Imprisoned, it is not. Its confines are Mother Earth and God's blue sky. Defenseless, it is not. With wings that can propel it to amazing altitudes and claws that can repel even the most vicious of predators, eagles are a rarity on any creature's menu.

One of these creatures has become the symbol of America, only because of its strength and ability to maintain independence. The eagle takes responsibility for its life because it must; the oyster is at the mercy of surrounding forces because it's impossible for it to be responsible. Each creature must live by its own code; it has no other choice.

OYSTER OR EAGLE?

Human beings have choices! People can choose to be oysters. The world is full of people who have shifted responsibility for their lives to their parents, spouses, siblings, offspring or friends. And as long as others willingly assume that responsibility, these people will continue to act irresponsibly. Of course, if and when others refuse to accept this responsibility, these people might find themselves at the mercy of the forces that surround them. Depending on their situations, they might be powerless to stop themselves from sliding alive down the throats of mediocrity, bankruptcy, prison terms, obesity, divorce, alcoholism, drug addiction, et al.

But people can choose to be eagles, if they dare. True, being responsible is not always easy. Sometimes, it's downright difficult and taxing to both body and soul. But there are rewards. Eagles fly as high as they like. And they don't slide down the throats of anyone or anything.

Sure, life isn't always easy for eagles. But what would it be worth to you to be able to fly? Not like an eagle, of course. I'm talking about the flight of the spirit that accompanies significant accomplishment—achievement that impresses yourself as well as others. Many people live their whole lives and never, ever know what it's like for their spirits to clear the ground, let alone soar.

I think the following passage from Morris L. West's **The Shoes Of A Fisherman** sums up quite nicely the demands of living a full life.

It costs so much to be a full human being that there are very few who have the enlightenment or the courage to pay the price . . . One has to abandon altogether the search for security and reach out to the risk of living with both arms. One has to embrace the world like a lover. One has to accept pain as a condition of existence. One has to court doubt and darkness as the cost of knowing. One needs a will stubborn in conflict, but apt always to total acceptance of every consequence of living and dying.

West makes a full life seem like risky business. It is. But so is anything worthwhile. People take on dogs as pets, knowing that in 10 to 15 years, they'll grieve over a loss. But they take pets anyway. People buy new cars, knowing it's only a matter of time before they are scratched, dented or wrecked. But they buy them anyway. Couples have children, knowing they can be snatched away by kidnappers, illnesses or accidents. They also know there's no guarantee the child will grow up to be a responsible adult. But they have children anyway.

These are just some of the more common risks that we take. But there are other risks offered by a complicated, ever-changing society such as ours.

Moving to a new town or state
Taking on a new job
Joining a social or civic club
Traveling abroad
Investing for the future
Buying a home
Enrolling in night school
Taking up a sport or hobby
Learning a second profession
Borrowing money
Loaning money
Flying

Of course, the list could go on and on. There is at least some degree of risk in everything. People brave rush-hour traffic to go to their jobs, knowing there's a chance they could be involved in an interstate pile-up that could make them history. But that's a risk we accept for being self-sufficient.

LIFE IS ONE RISK AFTER ANOTHER

In business, risk is the name of the game. The entrepreneur who would take ever-increasing risks (calculated gambles, not fool-hardy chances) stands the chance of being the most successful. True, he or she might also lose a bundle. Risk is risk; it doesn't always end satisfactorily. Any given action can produce varying results; only the results of inaction can be accurately predicted.

Likewise, life is full of risks. The more satisfying the life, the greater the risks, it often seems. It would almost appear that a person who would enjoy life to the fullest is the one most willing to take risks.

This means to get maximum enjoyment out of life, we all must become "entrepreneurs" of sorts. Webster's Dictionary defines entrepreneur as "one who organizes a business undertaking, assuming the risk for the sake of profit." In business, entrepreneurs risk time, money, creativity and effort to produce gain. We often must do the same thing to produce profitable life situations, be they financial or intrinsic by nature.

We must become entrepreneurs to prosper—both physically and emotionally—in our perpetually evolving society. If the prospect of taking such risks tends to make you nervous, take heart. As any successful entrepreneur will tell you, taking risks gets to be a habit. Creative entrepreneurs weigh all risks; they don't take them lightly, nor do they take risks where the loss is greater than the gain. But they take risks, and they keep taking risks until they die—or at least as long as they want to live worthwhile lives.

We can all become creative entrepreneurs. No matter our age, it's not too late. At any point in life, everyone has two things—hope and options. Creative entrepreneurs know how to combine the two to create for themselves pleasurable, meaningful existences. They learn from the past, but they don't live in it. They anticipate the future, but not at the expense of missing the present. Creative entrepreneurs know that "now" is the only moment that really counts, because "now" is the only moment they can act to improve their lives. Take a hint from Calvin Coolidge, the nation's 30th president.

> Of course we look to the past for inspiration, but inspiration is not enough. We must have action. Action can only come from ourselves; society, government, the state, call it what you will, cannot act; our only strength, our only security, lies in the individual. American institutions are builded on that foundation. That is the meaning of self-government, the worth and responsibility of the individual. In that America has put all her trust. If that fails, democracy fails, freedom is a delusion, and slavery must prevail.

In short, people's lives will be what they make them. It's a matter of personal choice. Only by accepting responsibility for their lives can people actually design them to their satisfaction—to achieve the satisfaction of independence and the freedom to do what they feel is important to them.

But let's be more specific and talk about you. What is important to you? If you've never asked yourself that question, now is as good a time as any to come up with an answer. If you have already defined what is of consequence, take caution. Many people have thrown their lives away pursuing what they thought was momentous, only to learn later (and usually too late) that what they had held important was really trivial in retrospect.

No matter what you think is important, I'd like you to be sure that you base your decision on a good self-image. That's the key to assessing our ability, performance, achievement level and happiness It's also the subject of the next chapter

CHAPTER HIGHLIGHTS

(1) To live a full life, there is no room for "straitjacket" thinking.

(2) Risk is an essential ingredient to a full, rewarding life.

(3) Most people are conditioned to fear success because they're conditioned to fear risk.

(4) We are the product of our choices.

(5) Adults are responsible—not victims. Responsibility doesn't come automatically. It must be cultivated. Often, people who don't develop it tend to blame others for their failings.

(6) To get maximum enjoyment out of life, we must become "entrepreneurs" who don't fear taking calculated risks.

MY PERSONAL ACTION PLAN

** The most important idea I gained from reading this chapter is: _____

_____ .

** My plan for using this idea is: _____

_____ .

** I will commit to this idea because: _____

_____

** The specific actions I will take to implement this idea are: _____

_____

_____ .

** The results I expect from my usage of this idea are: ___

_____

_____ .

Chapter Two

Forming the Core— a Strong Self-Image

All my life, I've been interested in what makes some people extremely successful, hoping that once I learned the secret, I could become extremely successful, too. So I researched the lives of great people and read the works of great psychologists, and it wasn't long before I discovered this valued trait. But I came to realize this feature that leads to success is also the same quality that makes some people mundane and mediocre—even downright sorry.

Assuming that I fell in a category somewhere between sorry and extremely successful, I deduced that I already had this quality, and so does everyone who has ever lived. So the bad news was that I already had what it took to be successful, but it wasn't working. But the good news? I could change it—mold it—to make it work.

This quality that plays a significant role in success or failure is an individual's self-image. Mahatma Gandhi had one. So did Adolph Hitler. One sought to free a race of people; the other sought to eliminate one. Both were motivated by their self-images.

Self-image is a mentally constructed picture of who a person is and what he or she can accomplish. Similarly, it's the motivating factor for the person's choice of actions, since behavior most often is consistent with self-image. For example, most skid row bums don't have bank accounts because they spend all the money they can beg, borrow or steal on booze. They don't "see" themselves saving money, because they have a stronger image of themselves as chronic drunks. Similarly, a successful business executive isn't likely to be seen hot-rodding down Main Street in a souped-up sedan that most people wouldn't have as a gift. The executive likely will have a different self-image, opting instead for a prestigious car that the masses can only envy.

Self-image is the reason some people are ill at ease with formal wear and others are uncomfortable in jeans. It plays a large part in deciding what we'll do for a living, where we'll live and how much our houses will cost. We consult our self-images when we consider joining churches and social or civic organizations. It plays a large part in determining our clothing and hair styles—even our personal hygiene. Self-image is the deciding factor whether we command respect or allow others to abuse us. If we feel we don't deserve any better, we'll be satisfied with shabby treatment from others.

SELF-IMAGE CAN BE "SEEN"

Self-image goes deeper still. It manifests itself in a person's physical appearance. People who are fat actually see themselves as fat people, or at least they can't see themselves as being thin.

Dr. Maxwell Maltz was a successful plastic surgeon who recognized the significance of self-image, which he detailed in his book **Psychocybernetics.** Through experiences with his patients, he discovered that all people have a "mental blueprint or picture" of themselves, and they chose their actions and behaviors based on that image. In many cases, when Maltz performed surgery to remove scars or correct deformities, he noted that the patient's self-image improved dramatically within a relatively short period of time. As a result, so did their actions and behaviors. That led Maltz to conclude that individuals can improve their lives by improving their self-images.

Personal appearance is a major indicator of self-image. People who don't care about the way they look probably won't care much about themselves in general. That's why, at least in the United States, body shape might be the prevalent method for gauging a person's self-image. Of course, that's a general statement. There will be out-of-shape people who will like themselves, just as there will be physically fit people who don't. But, as a rule, people who like themselves and see themselves as valuable people will take care of their bodies, while people with poor self-images either will neglect or abuse them.

Let's take a look at two studies conducted by Psychology Today magazine. The studies deal with the percentage of study respondents who are dissatisfied with the shapes of their bodies. The first study was taken in 1972, and the second was conducted in 1985.

Psychology Today Study

1972	Men	Women	1985	Men	Women
Height	13%	13%		20%	17%
Weight	35	48		41	55
Muscle Tone	25	30		32	45
Overall Face	8	11		20	20
Breast/Chest	18	26		28	32
Abdomen	36	50		50	57
Hips and Upper Thighs	12	49		21	50
Overall Appearance	15	25		34	38

Notice that the percentages from 1972 to 1985 increased in every category for both men and women. This means that an increasing number of people are becoming dissatisfied with their appearances.

This increased dissatisfaction might result from the 1980's emphasis on physical fitness. It also might reflect still strong trends for leisure and sedentary lifestyles—trends that sociologists say are expected to become even stronger during the 1990's.

Actually, the reasons are unimportant. The results are the problem. If this survey reflects an accurate sampling, then it's safe to say that more than one-third of American adults are displeased with their appearances, and likely suffer from poor self-images as a result. I believe this is a safe conclusion. Consider that the study also stated that 45% of female respondents and nearly one-third of the male respondents said they would consider cosmetic surgery as a means of improving their physical appearance. Obviously, that's an expensive and last-resort measure most people wouldn't even consider unless it was seen as a means of improving their self-images.

YOUR SELF-IMAGE IS WHAT YOU MAKE IT

A self-image is somewhat like a brain—everybody has one. It's how the self-image is developed that makes the difference in a person's life. And the "secret" is simple. Load a brain with valuable information and exercise it by solving problems, and the brain will become a powerful tool. Fill it with trivia and allow it to remain idle, and the brain will become a piece of junk. Likewise, people who see themselves as competent and productive will likely behave accordingly, while those who lack self-confidence and view themselves as inept will act accordingly, too.

In other words, a person can be strengthened or handicapped by self-image. But unlike a person with a physical handicap beyond his or her control, a handicap rooted in self-image is reversible. For example, take the person who says, "I could never learn math." Chances are good that he or she has never really tried, or that someone significant said that math was a problem subject for this person, who believed it and started avoiding it. Likewise for the person who is shy and retiring. Perhaps he or she has never really made an effort to mingle, or has been repeatedly classified by someone noteworthy as being socially inept. Personally, I viewed myself as unimaginative and uncreative. I have since dispelled this aspect of my self-image, and I am now quite proud of my creative thought process.

People accept what they and others think about them. They don't even have to like their critics; they only have to respect them. Many times, this respect comes naturally with parents, siblings, bosses and peers, even if admiration doesn't exist.

This is one reason why it's been said that if your friends constantly put you down, find a new set of friends, because you are what you think you are, regardless of how you come to think it. Despite your potential, you will always and only be how you act. As Jean-Paul Sartre said, "To do is to be."

SELF-IMAGE INFLUENCES PERFORMANCE

Let me explain with a chapter out of my life. As a child, I did more than dream about becoming a good basketball player. I worked hard at becoming one. After all, the great concept on which America was founded is that if you work hard, you'll succeed. And if you don't succeed, it's because you're not working hard enough.

In retrospect, I can say with all objectivity that I don't know anyone who worked harder than I did to become a good basketball player. In the heat of the summer, I dribbled and shot until my sweat covered the court. In the dead of the winter, I would shovel snow off outdoor courts to clear a playing area. I would practice for two hours prior to a game, play the game, then practice afterward, sometimes keeping at it well after midnight, bouncing the ball by moonlight.

After such long-term, intensive practice, you might think that I got good at shooting the basketball. But I didn't. In fact, I was so bad that I could sit in a rowboat in the middle of the ocean, shoot a basketball and still miss the water!

Finally, I came to realize that perhaps working harder wasn't the solution. Perhaps I needed to work smarter instead of harder. After all, it has been said that some of the poorest people in the world, financially speaking, have been some of the hardest working people. Successful people work smart. They continually are on the lookout for ways to increase their effectiveness.

For me to work smarter on the hard court, I decided to strengthen my skills via imagination combined with practice, rather than mere practice alone. After all, what benefit is there to practice if a person practices incorrectly? The resulting substandard performance will reinforce the person's self-image—in this case, that of a would-be basketball player in need of improvement.

But what if, before practice, I envisioned myself making the shots in my mind. Would it have any affect on my performance? It would. And, as I found out, it did. I first applied this principle while playing in a summer basketball league after graduating from college. At tryouts, I was agape, marveling at the size and extraordinary skills of these athletes. I was too slow and couldn't shoot fish in a barrel, let alone a basketball.

Or at least I **thought** I couldn't, and that's where my problem rested. Although I had spent untold numbers of hours practicing, I never got past my automatic assumption that I was incapable of performing well, and that's what made the difference. But after being coached by a friend who sold me on the power of imagination, I started to visualize myself playing basketball like a pro.

Did I become a pro? Not by a long shot. But I did make the leagues. And instead of scoring my typical eight to 10 points per game—an average player can hit that many almost by accident—I scored 29, 27 and 25 points for each of the three successive games of the championship series, which we won, thank you.

I had scored more points in three nights than I did my entire senior year of high school. What happened? I had no arm or eye transplant that made me perform better. I didn't even increase my time spent in practice. Imagination was the key. Instead of working harder, I started working smarter. I changed my self-concept, or the image of my personal basketball ability, and I got results. No, I didn't become a pro, but I can't help but wonder if I could have, had I discovered the power of imagination much earlier in my life.

Now that I know the power of visualization, I won't forget it. It can be applied to any endeavor or skill. If you want to be more competent, witty, clever, graceful, skillful or proficient, start by imagining yourself as being that way. Naturally, you'll need practice at anything you would master. But the first step is imagining yourself as you want to be.

For example, I fantasized about becoming a professional speaker long before I became one. For the longest time, I did not pursue the possibility of building a career as a speaker, simply because I didn't see myself as a speaker. But I changed my self-image through continued imagery. I began to see myself as a speaker. As a result, I started making serious efforts to build a speaking career, and I became successful. The power of imagination and self-image made the difference.

THE BRAIN RESPONDS TO IMAGINATION

Imagination is powerful, because the subconscious mind cannot distinguish between real and imagined experience. When watching motion pictures, do you ever wonder why your palms sweat when you watch trapeze artists perform? How about the tingly feeling you get when watching passionate love scenes, or the goose-pimples that bulge when you're watching a cut-and-stab flick. You know it's fiction. You know the actors are in no danger of falling—either to the ground, in love or victim to the killer. But you've become so engrossed in the story that your subconscious responds to it. You cry when the protagonist gasps "the final breath," even though you know he or she is really alive and well and has just signed a contract to do a new film.

Likewise, responses from the subconscious can be triggered through imagination. If you can imagine yourself performing successfully in a given endeavor, you can improve your chances of achieving that level of performance. You will have strengthened your self-image by mentally acquainting yourself with the taste of success. As a result, you'll be better able to "see" yourself succeeding. And when you try, your actual performance will likely improve, because your self-confidence was raised through imagination.

Learn from my mistakes as a would-be basketball player. Practice without the appropriate successful image is a waste of time. But armed with a clear image of success, practice is a means of bringing that image to reality.

SOURCES OF SELF-IMAGE

How do people form their self-images. Certainly, it's rarely done consciously. Let's look at the many factors that can influence a person's self-image.

(1) **Nicknames.** Nicknames generally result from a person's negative features. Children who grow up being called "Fatty," "Four-Eye," "Pigface," "Dummy" and "Spastic" often become self-conscious, defensive people.

(2) **People.** As we've already seen, a significant peer's opinion can carry a lot of weight with an individual, regardless of whether the opinion is true. Parents,

siblings, coaches, and teachers can play an important part in the building of a person's self-image.

(3) **Skills and abilities.** People tend to focus on what they can't do rather on what they can accomplish. They tend to compare themselves to people who have developed the skills they lack. As a result, these people feel they don't "measure up" to their peers, and they devalue themselves. Of course, no one can measure up to the strengths of all the individuals they know. To even think otherwise invites conflict.

(4) **Personal differences.** Many underprivileged young people feel they're not as good as those who have many advantages. Ironically, many overprivileged children feel they're not as good as their poorer peers who grew up without such benefits. It almost seems as if we sometimes look for reasons to kick ourselves.

(5) **Society's message.** All societies have their codes. America functions on a work ethic. The harder you work, the more valuable you are. As a result, people who "march to the beat of a different drummer" might feel inferior if their lives don't revolve around their jobs.

(6) **Media.** This is a powerful influence. It seems that the media's message is "Be slender, sexy and beautiful." Virtually anyone with access to expensive wardrobes and professional cosmetologists can look sexy. Although keeping a slender figure is admirable from the standpoint of health, "sexy" and "beautiful" is in the eye of the beholder—not the media.

(7) **Handicaps.** People with handicaps—especially those that are disfiguring—often feel "unworthy" of success. And that's a shame, because it's been proven

that handicapped workers often perform just as well—
if not better—than their able-bodied co-workers.

(8) **Grading systems.** I guess they're necessary to gauge
a student's performance, but they do not relate to a
person's potential, nor do they encourage growth. Although a student who "fails" might be extremely capable in a non-academic field, he or she might always
carry the scars of a self-image that was wounded in
the classroom. Grading systems exist also in business
and industry. Individuals are graded on how well they
perform. Oftentimes faults **must be** found by supervi-
sors.

(9) **Day-to-day experiences.** It's the little things in life
that people tend to remember—both positive and negative. Scorn, ridicule and rejection can make strong
impressions. So can positive events. Steve Morris was
a blind kid who sat in the back of the class with the
rest of the handicapped students during the 1950's.
No one gave him much thought until the day the class
hamster escaped from its cage. Teacher and students
were beside themselves until blind Steve came to the
rescue. With his acute sense of hearing, he quickly
located the lost pet and became a hero. Steve never
forgot that day, which proved to be a pivotal point
in the forming of his self-image. And, by the way,
"Stevie" changed his surname from Morris to Wonder
and made recording history at the age of 12.

(10) **Our own impatience.** Somehow, it always seems to
take less time to degenerate than it does to improve.
Sometimes, we kick ourselves for not improving or
developing as fast as we think we should. It's a case
where we are our own worst enemies.

As you can see, there are many factors that affect our self-images. Be aware of how they affect yours and work to strengthen it by rejecting negative input.

HOW DO YOU STRENGTHEN YOUR SELF-IMAGE?

Perhaps the best way to strengthen a self-image is by being aware of the "vultures" that feed off it. These vultures are nothing more than the negative concepts that people with low self-images nourish over time. Let's examine them.

(A) **Feeding on negatives.** Everybody's life has its negative, embarrassing, shameful and regretful moments. People with positive self-images just don't dwell on them. They learn from their mistakes and proceed with life. People with negative self-images continue to kick themselves, long after the actual incident has passed. This accomplishes only guilt and anger—two negative emotions that can erode a self-image even more.

(B) **We apologize for our weaknesses.** Everyone has weaknesses. If everyone apologized for them, nobody would ever get anything done. I'm not saying you shouldn't work to strengthen your weaknesses. But don't dwell on them. You owe apologies to no one for what you aren't and things you can't do. Continuing apology is self-demeaning.

(C) **Inability to accept praise.** People with low self-images often can't handle compliments and praise. If someone tells them they've done a good job, they'll spend the

29

next 27 minutes explaining how anyone could have done just as well. If someone compliments them on their clothes, they'll immediately devalue the compliment by devaluing the clothes. Of course, in so doing, the person devalues the one giving the compliment. A person who cannot accept praise says, in effect, "You're patronizing me," to the person who would offer a compliment.

Vultures consume a positive self-image by attacking six areas of human qualities—creativity, sexuality, physical appearance and abilities, family relationships, social life and social skills and intelligence. And it's easy to see how low marks in those areas can adversely effect a person's self-image.

Once the concept of self-image is understood, we can work to raise its level to enhance our abilities and performance. And this can best be done by getting rid of the vultures. It would be nice if you could kill them. But vultures, unfortunately, are indestructible. But you can make them embarrassed to show their faces, however, by plucking their feathers—one by one. Make them naked, and they'll fly away. Here's how that is done.

(1) **Accept yourself—faults as well as strengths.** People with positive self-images admire themselves, and they have faith in their abilities. Only then are they free to admire and respect others. This doesn't mean they are conceited. But it does mean they don't feed on negative thoughts about themselves and others.

(2) **Take responsibility.** An elderly gentleman gave college graduates a wise piece of advice: don't ask; just act. It is easier to apologize later than it is to beg for permission first. Of course, you must stand responsible for your actions, but that's part of being an adult. In many cases, asking permission is abdicating responsibility,

30

which amounts to turning over control of your life to someone else. Of course, there are some cases where permission is necessary. You can't parade down Main Street without a permit. You'd best not take a week off from work without prior explanation. And it's only common courtesy to clear plans with friends and family members if the plans affect them. But in situations that call for independent action, act. Don't seek permission when it's not necessary. It devalues your self-esteem.

(3) **Focus on the positives.** It's easy to focus on what is going wrong in our lives, what we don't have and what we're unable to do. But it's more productive and less stressful to focus on the positives—the things that are going right, what we have and what we're able to do. It builds a healthier self-image and makes us more thankful to be alive.

(4) **Get experience.** If you're unsure of yourself in a given endeavor, practice. Get experience. You can read all the books you'd like and talk with all the experts you know, but nothing beats experience as a teacher. At times when you can't get experience, you can always experience an event or endeavor in your mind. Self-image is rooted in the subconscious. Visualize your success. This is the process of Psychocybernetics that I used to become a better speaker and basketball shooter.

(5) **Avoid people who put you down.** It's hard to keep a positive self-image when key people in your environment constantly criticize you. If your ''friends'' don't treat you with respect, find a new set of friends. If your boss verbally abuses you, find a new job. If family members take delight in deflating your ego, keep your distance—and, when you're with them, strengthen your resolve not to let them get you down.

Feeling good about yourself is not only a nice way to pass the time of your life; it's also the key to success and achievement. Human beings are such superb creations that we don't recognize our potential for greatness. Self-image most often is the make-or-break quality for human beings.

Yet, this must be one of the best kept secrets in the world, because there seem to be so many miserable people. When I taught high school, I was amazed by the number of young people who were adamant about remaining ignorant. Don't get me wrong, I have had some wonderful students as well. But "I'm not going to learn, and you can't make me" seemed to be the motto of some. Talk about being your own worst enemy! People who take pride in ignorance eventually will find themselves with little to be proud of.

A study conducted by the Carnegie Institute of Technology during the 1970's revealed that there are three components critical to success in any endeavor. The first is knowledge. The second is skill, or the ability to apply knowledge to produce desired results. Ironically, those two components contribute only 15% of what an individual can accomplish. This means that 85% of what an individual can do is based on the third component—attitude. Obviously, this is a vital ingredient to success, and we'll discuss it thoroughly in the next chapter.

But how is attitude formed? My research and experience indicates that it's the product of an individual's self-image. A person who feels good about himself will have a positive attitude, while a person who feels ineffective and worthless probably will have a negative attitude. So if 85% of what an individual is able to accomplish is based on self-image, then why don't we spend more time developing it in schools and in the workplace. We'll spend billions of dollars developing people's skills and abilities, which comprise the other 15% of productive action. Yet, if we invested the same amount or even less in the development of self-image, America's results could be significantly increased.

I hope I've sold you on the significance and power of a strong self-image. If yours is weak, I hope you'll take my advice to strengthen it. And if yours is strong, I hope you'll strengthen it, anyway. It's mostly a matter of attitude. If you need help in that department, check out the next chapter.

CHAPTER HIGHLIGHTS

(1)   Self-image is the personal quality that plays a significant role in success and failure. It's a person's mentally constructed picture of who and what he or she is or can accomplish.

(2)   Self-image manifests itself in a person's physical appearance. People who don't care about the way they look probably won't care much about themselves in general.

(3)   A person can be strengthened or handicapped by his or her self-image. But unlike a person with a physical handicap beyond his or her control, a handicap rooted in self-image is reversible.

(4)   When used positively, the power of imagination, or visualization, can lead to success. The subconscious mind cannot distinguish between real and imagined experience. Feeding it messages of success can lead to success.

(5)   There are many factors that come into play when an individual's self-image is formed. Work to strengthen your self-image by rejecting negative input.

(6)   Be aware of the "vultures" that feed upon self-images. Stop feeding on negatives, apologizing for weaknesses, rejecting praise and compliments. Eliminate the vultures

by accepting yourself, taking responsibility, focus on positives, get experience and avoid people who put you down.

(7) It has been estimated that 85% of what we do is based on our attitudes, and our self-images play an important role in choosing our attitudes.

MY PERSONAL ACTION PLAN

** The most important idea I gained from reading this chapter is: _____

_____ .

** My plan for using this idea is: _____

_____ .

** I will commit to this idea because: _____

_____ .

** The specific actions I will take to implement this idea are: _____

_____

_____ .

** The results I expect from my usage of this idea are: ____

_____

_____ .

Chapter Three

Life Is a Matter of Attitude

Before we really get into this chapter, I'd like you to pause for a few seconds to think about the people you admire. Perhaps you know them personally, through the media or because they made history. How you know them is unimportant. I want you to think of why you admire them. What is it about these people that makes you admire them? I suggest you jot down their names and qualities you admire.

Of course, I don't know your choices. But in most cases, I'll bet the reason you admire them relates to their attitudes more than it does their skills and abilities. Some of the most talented and competent people alive are also some of the biggest jerks. And I don't care how effective a person with a poor attitude might be; with a strong, positive attitude, he or she can be even more effective. A person with a good attitude has a better chance of developing strengths and abilities than does someone with a negative attitude.

Remember, psychologists say 85% of our accomplishments are directly related to our attitudes.

Let me offer another piece of my past that tends to support this theory. When I was a boy, I enrolled at a basketball camp, a summer session with basketball pros to help young people improve their skills on the hardcourt. It was there that I met a very significant role model—Indiana University's basketball coach, Bobby Knight.

As you might already know, Coach Knight has quite a reputation for bizarre behavior at times, which is not completely undeserved. In fact, I had the opportunity to experience the wrath of his anger at a summer basketball camp when I was 13 years old. On that particular day, I had failed to complete an assigned drill to his satisfaction.

The first thing I knew, I found myself looking down on Knight. No, he didn't fall to his knees, begging me to complete the drill correctly. Instead, he lifted me into the air. An instant later, I was looking up to Knight from the asphalt where he had dropped me— if "slammed" isn't a more appropriate term.

I hurt—in more ways than one. But it was a momentous occasion in my life. There was no denying the fact that my idol had used me to vent his frustration. But I had a decision to make. How was I going to view the situation?

I could have viewed it negatively by thinking, "This guy is crazy. I didn't enroll in this camp to be brutalized." Or I could have seen the situation as a positive experience by thinking, "This man is trying his best to make me the best I can become, and I really respect his efforts and judgment." That was the outlook I chose, and I became a better basketball player on account of it. (As a matter of fact, defense became the major aspect of my game. I was our team's defensive specialist and was even named to the Honorable Mention All League team. And remember, I couldn't shoot!)

Now, I don't know Knight's motivation for the action. I'd like to think he really was trying to inspire me to improve my performance.

But, on the other hand, he could have been a five-ply jerk who didn't like my looks. But his motivation wasn't important. **What was important was my reaction to it.**

Being slammed to the asphalt didn't improve my knowledge or my skills. By the same token, it didn't detract from them either. But had I chosen to be resentful, I might have protested by refusing to polish my skills. And, of course, that would have adversely affected my performance. So you can see how important attitude is to the development of knowledge and skills.

And that's what this chapter is about. We seldom can control what happens to us in life, but we always—repeat, always—can control our reaction to it. It's a matter of having the right attitude. And the message of this chapter is simple: no matter what happens to you in life, it's better to learn from it than to burn from it. Anger is not a positive emotion, and prolonged anger is non-productive and unhealthy—emotionally, mentally and, eventually, even physically. With a little soul-searching, virtually any situation that might provoke anger or resentment can be viewed positively.

GOOD DAY OR BAD DAY?

Noted psychologist Viktor Frankl was a German Jew who spent time during World War II in a concentration camp, where he made some interesting discoveries about human nature. He noted in that vile environment that his imprisoned peers tended to react one of three ways to their plights. They could lash out at their captors and be killed on the spot; they could resign themselves to their cruel fates and wither away emotionally before expiring physically; or they could accept the reality of their circumstances and make the best of them by helping others cope with the dilemma. The people who chose the last option had a fighting chance at survival.

Now let's take a moment to imagine a concentration camp—a place where people lived, slept, ate (if they were lucky) and exercised their bodily functions in the same area. Those who died might have been considered fortunate. The survivors carried scars that would never heal. They had witnessed wholesale slaughter of their peers— in many instances of their own family members. I believe that days when experiences like those occur could easily qualify as "bad days" by anyone's definition.

Yet, if *Frankl and others could refuse to let such days prevent them from functioning positively, why do we often let days marked by decidedly milder misfortunes blow our attitudes? Possibly because our attitudes aren't in the proper shape in the first place.

What makes a day good or bad for you? Some people moan every Monday morning when, after enjoying a weekend break, they're faced with another five days "at the grind." Yet, others appreciate Mondays for the opportunity to earn another week's income. Some people view rain as a "downer," while others appreciate it because it nourishes the earth, contributes to healthy crops and replenishes our water supply. Some people view hot, sunny days as oppressive, while others view them as opportunities to get half-naked and wash their cars, not at all minding if they get wet in the process. Some people hate mowing their lawns, while others enjoy the opportunity for prolonged, mild exercise.

I could ramble on, but I think my point is clear. Short of the untimely and unexpected death of a loved one, virtually any situation can be viewed as good or bad. I've known people who were devastated upon breaking a relationship or losing a job, only to discover later that the incident served as the turning point of their lives. They were forced to make other plans that produced better, more rewarding situations.

The next time you have an exceptionally good or bad day, make a list of the day's events. You might find that "good days" and "bad days" are just perceptions of the events, rather than reality. Again, this doesn't mean that everything can be great with the right attitude. I would be hard pressed to find something good in discovering that a friend had contracted a terminal disease or my condominium had burned to the ground. But we can certainly expedite our periods of adjustment to unfortunate events through a positive mental attitude. Instead of spending the rest of our lives being remorseful, we can learn to make the best of our misfortunes and get on with life.

BORED?

If good and bad days are a matter of personal perception, then what about boredom and excitement? Doesn't the same principle apply. You bet it does. For example, a rousing rendition of Richard Wagner's "Overture To Tannhauser" might be exciting to people who enjoy classical music. But to the person who would rather be at a rock concert, the overture would be painfully boring.

Tastes in clothes, music, art and people are a matter of personal choice. This means that when people are bored, it's likewise a matter of choice. They actually choose to be bored. They decide not to enjoy their situations, rather than try to find something about them to like.

The best cure for boredom is to make use of your senses. When used fully, sight, hearing, taste, touch and smell can reveal a new and exciting dimension to any situation perceived as boring.

For example, suppose it's a Saturday, and you have absolutely no plans for the day. You don't even have any ideas for what to do. Looks like it's going to be a boring day. Not if you make the right choices.

If you choose to be bored by the prospect of a dull day, then you will be. On the other hand, if you choose to view the opportunity as an open day during which you can do anything you want, you can set the stage for excitement.

Use your senses. Go outside and feel the sunshine, or open a window and listen to the rain as it hits the ground. Smell the freshness of the morning air, the fragrance of blooming pear blossoms and the scent of freshly mown grass. If it's a hot day, take a drive in the country. Give the air conditioner a break and open the car windows. Feel the breeze rushing inside as you drive on open roads. Enjoy the bouquet of honeysuckle and assorted wild flowers. Catch a whiff of tar and asphalt as you cross a bridge or railroad track, or sniff the crisp smell of gasoline as you pass a country service station.

The world seems different when we use all of our senses. In fact, I believe that's a major reason why people suffer depression; they don't make full use of their senses. We tune out many fine moments. We don't savor the taste of a good steak, a juicy orange or a glass of chocolate milk. We don't stop and listen—I mean really listen—to the symphonies of singing birds, chirping crickets and heavy traffic. We don't appreciate the budding leaves, or even the falling ones for that matter.

For example, a heavy snowfall for people in the northeast is no big deal. It's a common occurrence—one that most northern residents accept as business as usual. But in the South, a significant snowfall becomes a joyous occasion—simply because it's a relatively rare event. When a heavy snowfall materializes, people's routine lives tend to go "on hold." School is canceled, and so are some work shifts. People take delight in watching the snow fall. Although they know the roads might be hazardous when they finally venture out in the snow, they often are sorry to see it end.

The difference is the interpretation of the events. Of course, I'm not saying that Southerners necessarily are more in tune with their senses. When it comes to warm, pleasant days conducive to swimming and sunbathing, the reverse is probably true. Perhaps Northerners savor such days more than their neighbors to the south, simply because there are fewer of these days above the Mason-Dixon line.

CREATE AN ENVIRONMENT FOR EXCITEMENT

Since excitement is a matter of perception, it stands to reason that excitement can be created. It's not necessary to wait for it to happen. Of course, people plan vacations and long weekends for an exciting change of pace, but there are other ways of creating excitement.

You can begin by changing your patterns. People often become bored with routine, regardless of what it involves. But there's no law that says it can't be changed. Instead of waking up at 7:15, why not wake up at 6:15, or 5:15? Try something new for breakfast—especially if you're accustomed to skipping the meal. Do something exciting with the extra time you've created by spending less time in bed. Read a book, write a letter, take a walk, exercise, watch a good movie on your videocassette recorder . . . the options are numerous.

If you can manage it, rearrange your work hours. If you're accustomed to having nights free, try taking a morning off. Why not work a morning and an evening and take off an afternoon? It would be a perfect time for a romp in the park or a dip in the nearest swimming pool.

As Oscar Wilde said, "Consistency is the last refuge of the unimaginative." A certain degree of routine is necessary for a stable life, but too much of it can become monotonous. Variety is the spice of life.

MAKE A LIST OF THANKFULS

I have found that many people have problems counting their blessings. They feel they don't have any to count. If that's how you feel, let me make a suggestion: tomorrow morning when you wake up, immediately walk to your nearest mirror and take a good look at yourself. I'll bet you'll be thankful for the fact that you won't look like that all day.

All jokes aside, the average person has plenty for which to be thankful. If you have heat in your dwelling and carpet on your floor, you've got more than many people in the world. Be thankful that you have running hot water, a clean towel and clean clothes. Many people don't. If you can sit down to breakfast, be thankful that you're not a member of an underdeveloped country where any food—not just breakfast—is a rarity. And if you can afford to have breakfast out, why, what a luxury! Whenever I meet people who aren't thankful for these small but significant amenities, I ask them if they'd like to trade places with someone like Ray Charles or Stevie Wonder. They're gifted musicians who are financially independent, but they never get the pleasure of seeing the sun rise and set—let alone viewing the countless other wonders of nature.

Don't get me wrong. I'm not saying that the average person doesn't have problems. I'm just saying that perhaps we too often let our problems overpower our positives. Don't be so preoccupied with life's bad aspects that you forget to appreciate its good ones.

FOCUS ON STRENGTHS AND ACCOMPLISHMENTS

One good way to keep a positive attitude is by focusing on your personal positives—your strengths and accomplishments. As a seminar leader, I too often meet people who do just the opposite— they focus on their weaknesses and their failures. They erode their own self-confidence. Inadequacy and ineffectiveness becomes a mind-set, and their attitude suffers. As a result, they won't attempt endeavors that could prove to be growing experiences because they fear failure. They refuse to "create possibilities," or subject themselves to experiences that would cause them to stretch their abilities and take risks. In short, they get stuck in a rut, which is nothing more than a grave with different dimensions!

Making a list of personal strengths and accomplishments is the best way to reverse this negative situation. By focusing on positive points, a person can create a mindset for growth and success.

As human beings, we're still learning how far we can go. Physiologists thought it impossible for a person to run a mile in four minutes. They thought the heart would literally explode under such strain. But British athlete Roger Bannister proved them wrong in 1954 by running the four-minute mile. Within months, others had done it, too. When they saw that it actually could be done, they stopped setting limitations on their abilities.

Negative attitudes about ourselves places limitations on our abilities. By focusing on strengths and past accomplishments, we can break through these limitations and become more effective.

ATTITUDE CHANGING TIPS

If your attitude needs a good "shot in the arm," or a major overhaul, you might benefit from these tips.

(1) **Create an environment conducive to a good attitude.**
Decorate your dwelling in stimulating colors. Listen to motivational experts on cassette tapes. Associate with people who have good attitudes, and avoid those who don't. Attitudes are contagious, whether they are positive or negative. Small-minded people can frustrate you, while broad-minded people challenge you to grow. Be selective in what you watch on television. Clip cartoons and art that express your outlook on life. I have a collection featuring Odie, the dog in "Garfield," the popular

cartoon and comic strip character, who always empha-
sizes the importance and positive impact of hugs. Display photographs and posters of your role models. In
my apartment, I have posters of Bobby Knight, baseball
great Pete Rose and the Three Stooges—the latter to
remind me to laugh. Be a creative entrepreneur by taking
a stand in your life. Give yourself cues in your environment to help produce the kind of attitude you would
like to maintain or adopt.

(2) **Focus on your uniqueness.** All of us are unique individuals. There is no one in the world exactly like you.
Yet, many people develop poor attitudes for this very
reason. They feel they are different from the crowd.
In high school, this very feeling drives teenagers crazy,
because they think there is something wrong with them.
From discussions with teens in my psychology classes,
their number one complaint by far is that they feel
there is something wrong with them or that they are
inadequate. When I conducted my "Success With
Mess" program, a self-improvement course for high
school students, I tried to free them from that concept.
Those who were freed took on a much different frame
of mind. It was very, very gratifying to watch them
"blossom" as people. They developed healthier attitudes and self-images (the two are intertwined, of
course). The same holds true for adults at times. I see
very little difference between an adult and a teen-ager
in behavior patterns. But underneath the stronger facade,
the same insecurities often apply.

(3) **Don't complain about things you can or cannot
change.** Complaining about things within our power
to change is the best way to develop a self-defeating
attitude. Complaining about matters such as an undesir-

able job, a weight problem or unhealthy habits subtly reinforces that we have no control over our lives, which is wrong. We all have control over our lives; some of us choose not to exercise it. In those cases, complaining is often a paltry attempt at venting frustration that, unfortunately, most often leaves the person more frustrated than before. Devote your energies to correcting undesirable situations you can change.

Do you know who your best friend is? It's you, or at least it should be. You are the person you'll have to spend the rest of your life with. You are the person whose approval you'll seek most often. You are the person you must make happy throughout your life.

It distresses me to see people who are their own worst enemies. They tend to ruin anything good that might develop in their lives. Good friends don't make life unbearable and unpleasant for each other. And since people are their own best friends, they shouldn't make life unpleasant for themselves. Maintaining a positive attitude can help people make life more pleasant.

The first step for improving life is determining their ambitions. That's the subject of the next chapter.

CHAPTER HIGHLIGHTS

(1) Maximum effectiveness results from strong, positive attitudes.

(2) We seldom can control what happens to us in life, but we always can control our reaction to it. It's a matter of having the right attitude.

(3) Virtually any event can be viewed as good or bad. People with positive attitudes will try to find something good about the events of their lives.

(4) Boredom and excitement are matters of personal choice. It depends upon how people interpret a given event. What is exciting to one person might be boring to another. The best cure for boredom is to use your senses fully.

(5) Excitement can be created. Change your routine.

(6) Counting blessings can build a positive attitude.

(7) Build and maintain a positive attitude by focusing on personal strengths and accomplishments.

(8) Give your attitude a boost by creating an environment conducive to maintaining a positive attitude. Focus on your uniqueness, and don't complain about things you can change.

MY PERSONAL ACTION PLAN

** The most important idea I gained from reading this chapter is: _____

_____ .

** My plan for using this idea is: _____

_____ .

** I will commit to this idea because: _____

_____ .

** The specific actions I will take to implement this idea are: _____

_____

_____ .

** The results I expect from my usage of this idea are: ____

_____

_____ .

Chapter Four

Chart Your Future

If your future could be the way you wanted it to be, what would it be like?

Let's try a simple exercise. I call it a "60-second brainstorm." Supposing your future could be the way you'd like, think of all the things you dream about obtaining, achieving or accomplishing in your lifetime, and put it down on paper.

Now, to make sure you capture your most important dreams, let's try another 60-second brainstorm. Only this time, imagine that you only have a week to live. What dreams would you eliminate from the list? Are there any desires you would add to it?

Hopefully, you have longer than a week to live. Of course, the imaginary scenario was intended to make you think about what is most important to you. So if you took the time and trouble to form a list of your ideal future, I'll bet it looks good to you. And why shouldn't it? The list is a recording of the way you'd like for your future to be, if it could be any way that you want.

So my question to you is, why can't it be? Why can't the future be the way you would like? There's no reason your future can not be of your own making. In fact, there is no chance that your future won't be of your own making.

The future is not simply a set of events waiting to happen. It's not a life script with your name on it that you're predestined to follow. The future can and will be whatever you make it. Hopefully, it will be what you want it to be. For many people, it won't. It will be something that just happens. Only if fate is kind to them will their futures be pleasant.

What's the difference between people who make their futures and those who don't? The only significant difference is that people who make their own futures are willing to set and work toward challenging and rewarding ambitions.

THE POSSIBILITIES ARE ENDLESS

Ambitions are possibilities for our lives—nothing more, nothing less. They are the seeds of self-fulfillment and happiness. But whether they become reality depends on whether we establish and follow a plan of action.

To do that, we must know what is important. Perhaps the two 60-second brainstorms might have helped you visualize your desired future. If not, maybe an examination of various components of life can help you determine your ambitions. Let's examine some of the major ones.

(A) **Physical.** To chart your future, you must have one. There are three good ways to maximize chances that you'll have a future. One is to avoid dangerous situations, such as reckless driving. Two is to limit or eliminate certain vices that would jeopardize your health. And the third way to maintain good health is by engaging in moderate to vigorous exercise for 20 to 30 minutes, three to four times per week. By taking care of yourself, you can maximize the remainder of time you have left to pursue and achieve your ambitions. Of course, this area also could include ambitions to complete a triathlon or to develop a body that could adorn the cover of **Strength and Health** magazine. But for most people, maintaining a good weight level and taking care of the body itself is probably enough.

(B)   **Career.** Your career obviously will mean a great deal to you. Careers give us purpose, they help build our self-esteem and they provide us with income that we can apply toward necessities and desires. If you don't have any career ambitions, let me suggest that you might be in the wrong career, and I'd heartily advise you to look into the possibility of establishing another.

(C)   **Educational/intellectual.** Although we discussed that attitude plays a significant role in performance, that's not to understate the importance of knowledge. Knowledge not only makes performance possible, but it gives us the self-confidence that contributes to a positive attitude. People who desire to improve upon what they do should have educational goals to coincide with their ambitions for personal advancement.

(D)   **Financial.** If you want to be among the 3% of people who are self-sufficient upon retirement, then you might consider making plans regarding your finances. The same is true if you ever consider a major acquisition such as a home or your own business. Likewise if you want to take an extended cruise to some exotic tropical island. Whatever you want out of life will cost you something. Most of the time, it will be money.

(E)   **Emotional/spiritual.** Of course, there's more to life than money. Activities with our family and friends are important for our emotional development and satisfaction. Also, human beings are three-dimensional—physical, mental and spiritual, and the last category should not be overlooked by the person who wants to develop a full life.

(F) **Relationships.** This is the area that makes life worth living. Success without people to share it is painfully empty. No one is an island. We depend on effective interaction with others to build families, friendships and business associates. The person who can't build relationships probably won't be able to build a fulfilling life.

It's important to realize and clarify ambitions you have in all life areas. Before you can become successful, it's important to identify what success and fulfillment means to you. After all, if you don't identify your idea of success, how can you hope to reach it?

GETTING THERE

Of course, clarifying your concept of success is only the first step. The real work lies in bringing the idea to reality. Depending on your ambition, bringing it to reality can be extremely difficult.

But, as noted television minister and motivational speaker Dr. Robert Schuller says, "Yard by yard, life is hard; inch by inch, it's a cinch!" No matter how grand your ambition, you can break it down into a series of objectives that can guide you to success.

Let's assume that your ambition is to start your own business, but, at this point, you lack the experience and capital. Using this ambition, let me show you how it can be divided into a series of smaller objectives.

(1) **Long-range ambition.** This is the ambition itself—to start a business and make it successful. Of course, this might require a considerable amount of capital that you'd have to raise before starting the endeavor. Although time lengths for long-range ambitions can vary, they generally require 10 or more years to accomplish.

(2) **Intermediate ambition.** This might include earning a college degree or getting necessary experience to qualify you as an effective business person in your chosen field. Also, a good intermediate goal might be to amass a certain amount of capital to show that you're on your way to accumulating enough money. Time lengths can vary for intermediate ambitions, but they generally run three to five years.

(3) **Short-term ambition.** In this case, a short-term ambition might be enrolling in school, starting a job designed to give you experience and making a significant contribution to a fund earmarked for your new business start. Short-term ambitions generally run from about six months to a year.

When you break down your ambitions into a sequence of smaller objectives, it will be easier to achieve your ultimate desires. Rather than being overwhelmed by an enormous long-range ambition, you'll be focusing on a series of individual steps designed to bring the long-term ambition to reality.

THE POWER OF FOCUSING

People who are able to focus on their objectives most often are successful, because they concentrate on activities that will lead to successful accomplishment. By making the current objective their mission, they tend to avoid activities that don't apply to their ambitions.

For example, when I realized my ambition to write this book, I suddenly found myself focused on the project. When I wasn't actually working, I was busy researching, making notes and arranging facts and illustrations. I found there was little time for television, radio and a host of other activities in which I had been accustomed to indulging. As a result, I saw progress much faster, and my self-confidence increased with each successful endeavor.

So let me offer some tips on how to focus on an ambition for optimum results.

(1) **Write down ambitions, and read them daily.** I write my ambitions on three-by-five index cards. With one ambition per card, they're easy to handle and read. And by reading them every day, you'll remind yourself of their meaning in your life. Believe me, this step is important. Life is full of urgencies that can overshadow our ambitions if we're not careful. Daily reading keeps them uppermost in your mind.

(2) **Weed out insignificant activities.** It always seems we need more hours in the day. The only way we'll get them is by eliminating activities that aren't pertinent to our ambitions. Ask the question, is this activity helping me to reach my valued goals?

(3) **Reserve time for your most important ambitions.** If an ambition is worth pursuing, it's worth devoting time to. Set aside time in your life—preferably when you won't be interrupted—for the pursuit of your most driving ambitions.

(4) **Seek company of people with similar ambitions.** You can get a lot of support—not to mention ideas—from

people whose ambitions are similar to yours. Also, it's a good idea to read about people who have been successful in your chosen field. If possible, talk with them. You could learn something in a few minutes that otherwise might have taken months—if not years—to discover for yourself. You can't fly like an eagle if you associate with a bunch of turkeys!

(5) **Imagine that you already have achieved the ambition.** This goes back to the power of imagination that we discussed earlier. By visualizing yourself as successful, you'll send "success messages" to your brain. These messages will positively influence your self-image, which will encourage you to operate at peak performance. As a result, your chances of succeeding will be greatly increased.

(6) **Concentrate on short-term objectives.** People who concentrate on their long-term desires often become frustrated and give up. But people who concentrate on their short-term objectives usually become successful. By concentrating on the short term, the long-range ambition will take care of itself. If you find this difficult, try to recognize satisfaction in completing short-term objectives. For example, people who exercise only to improve the shapes of their bodies tend to become frustrated. After all, it takes bodies a long time to take on different shapes. But people who exercise because it makes them feel better will usually stick with it to reap the reward of a better-looking body.

(7) **Keep your eye on the prize.** The best way to maintain enthusiasm is by keeping in mind your desired reward. This also allows our built-in "success mechanisms" to go to work—working for us. When frustration and despair set in, renew your efforts by focusing on your

ultimate ambition. Post photographs of tangible items you aspire to own, such as cars, boats and homes or photographs of desired ends such as a sprinter breaking the tape, wearing a gold medal or sitting behind the desk as a CEO to help inspire you to achieve.

Focusing is critical to achieving your ambitions. If something is important enough to excite you, then it's important enough to receive your best efforts.

DON'T BREAK HABITS; REPLACE THEM

Some of your ambitions might involve lifestyles that have no room for habits you currently hold. For example, if you smoke three packs of cigarettes a day and have an ambition to compete in a triathlon, I'd say that you're going to have to give up something—either your cigarette habit or your ambition.

Bad habits can interfere with our ambitions. If upon arriving home, we habitually hit the couch and turn on the television, we can use a lot of time that might have been put to better use in a productive endeavor.

Unfortunately, bad habits are difficult to drop. People become accustomed to acting out a practice, and old habits die hard. But they won't put up as much of a fight if you replace them instead.

It all goes back to attitude. Instead of dropping a habit, why not start a new one? Don't focus on the loss of an accustomed practice. Instead, focus on the gain of a new one. Cultivate tastes for water instead of soft drinks, fruits instead of sweets, fresh vegetables instead of cigarettes, exercise instead of inactivity.

Habits can make or break us. And the power of bad habits is strong. But the power of good habits can help us succeed in our chosen endeavors. If you have habits that don't fit with your personal interpretation of success, find a good practice to put the bad one in its place—history.

THE LAW OF SMALL DIFFERENCES

When determining your ambitions, be realistic. Don't expect too much, too soon. The sheer burden of unrealistic expectations can frustrate you into inaction.

It's better to set **small, realistic and relatively easy to attain ambitions and increase them gradually,** rather than to set a large ambition, only to become discouraged and lose motivation. Small ambitions activate a positive self-image and our success mechanisms.

For example, many dieters set unrealistic weight-loss goals. They go on crash diets for weeks, only to cave in eventually and revert to their old eating habits. But consider the person who approaches weight loss differently. By cutting back on caloric intake by 100 calories per day, he or she can lose 10 pounds in a year. Cut back by 200 calories per day, and 20 pounds can be shed within 12 months.

One hundred to 200 calories is a relatively insignificant reduction in daily caloric intake. But given time, insignificant contributions can amount to impressive results.

In short, don't be afraid to think big. But don't be afraid to think small, either. Big ambitions can be realized through small efforts.

DESTINY: SUCCESS—AT WHAT?

All of God's creatures have ambitions. Most of them have only one overriding desire—survival. And beasts are pretty good at surviving. After all, you don't see many animals that suffer from mal-nutrition (unless they're penned and starved by their human keep-ers).

It just goes to show that all creatures were created to succeed. And that includes human beings. But are we not much more sophisti-cated than beasts? After all, we are the only living animals that can choose from many worthy goals, ranging from survival to self-fulfillment. We can also choose to pursue meaningless goals, if we desire. The choice is ours.

But once the choice is made and the pursuit becomes standard fare, the person generally will succeed. If an individual regularly invests money wisely, he or she will one day succeed at accumulating significant assets. On the other hand, if a person drinks a pint of whiskey every night, chances are good he or she will succeed at becoming an alcoholic.

People act the way they program themselves to act. The subcon-scious mind operates like a machine. It sends messages the individual has programmed it to send. If those messages are geared to success, the person will stand a good chance of succeeding. On the other hand, if those messages are related to failure, the person very possibly will fail.

People are destined to succeed at something. Whether we succeed at being a success or failure in our chosen endeavors depends on how ardently and frequently we pursue our ambitions and how well we use the time we can devote to them. If you need help in the time department, the next chapter should interest you.

CHAPTER HIGHLIGHTS

(1) People who make their own futures are willing to set and work toward challenging and rewarding ambitions.

(2) Fulfilling lives can be obtained by setting ambitions in different life areas, including physical, career, educational/intellectual, financial, emotional/spiritual and relationships.

(3) Ambitions can be realized by breaking them down into three categories—long-range, intermediate and short-term.

(4) Focus on your ambitions by writing them down and reading them daily, weeding out insignificant activities in your life, reserving time for them and seeking the company of people with similar ambitions. Also, imagine that you already have achieved the ambition, concentrate on short-term objectives and keep your eye on the prize.

(5) Don't try to break bad habits; replace them instead with good ones.

(6) When determining your ambitions, be realistic. Don't expect too much, too soon.

(7) People are destined to succeed at something. Whether we succeed at being a success or failure in our chosen endeavors depends on how ardently and frequently we pursue our ambitions.

MY PERSONAL ACTION PLAN

** The most important idea I gained from reading this chapter is: _____

_____ .

** My plan for using this idea is: _____
_____.

** I will commit to this idea because: _____
_____.

** The specific actions I will take to implement this idea
are: _____

_____

_____.

** The results I expect from my usage of this idea are: ___

_____

_____.

Chapter Five

As the Clock Ticks

The first law of science states that matter can neither be created nor destroyed. But what about time? Does the law apply to it. After all, time is not matter. It can neither be seen nor touched, and it doesn't take up space. So we can assume the law doesn't apply to time. Of course, that's a faulty assumption. Time might not be matter, but it certainly cannot be created or destroyed. All people have 24 hours per day at their disposal—no more and no less.

But can time be wasted? You bet it can. Studies show that most employees use only a fraction of an eight-hour day efficiently. Some estimates say that white-collar workers waste an hour for every hour of productivity. If those estimates are true—and I don't doubt them—think of how America's productivity could rise if employees would put time to better use.

Time passes at the same rate for everyone, regardless of who they are or where they live. Time might not be of matter, but it matters a great deal when it comes to realizing our ambitions, because a major difference between successful people and failures is the way they use time.

WHO CAN MANAGE TIME?

What would you do with one more hour per day? Let's consider the possibilities. You could apply the additional 60 minutes to work, leisure, exercise or your own pursuits. If you'd like, you could spend the extra hour in bed.

But we've already determined that time can't be created, so we can't really add an hour to our days. This means that time management is impossible. After all, there is no one on this planet who is able to alter time's length. Therefore, it's uncontrollable and, thus, unmanageable. Case closed.

Yet, it's still possible to "add," for all practical purposes, an hour or more to your day by putting your time to better use. Time management might be impossible, but self management isn't. By decreasing the time you devote to various obligations, you can effectively increase the amount of discretionary time at your disposal.

For example, suppose you must perform three tasks, each of which generally requires an hour. But suppose you find a way to accomplish each task within 45 minutes. This means you effectively "save" 15 minutes on each task. Totaled, you'll then have 45 minutes of discretionary time that you can devote to something else. (By the way, we tend to "fill" the time available to us for our goals and projects. For example, if we have an hour for a project, we tend to fill the hour. Given 30 minutes, we strive to do the same amount of work in less time, often being successful.)

That's what self-management is all about. True, your day is only going to last 24 hours, no matter how much or how little you do. But by making the most efficient use of your time, you'll be able to schedule more activities into your days. As a result, you'll be more productive and effective—two qualities that always are in demand with businesses. But, more importantly, by using time efficiently, you can sooner achieve your objectives. And, when your objectives hinge on deadlines, efficient use of time often makes the difference between whether you achieve them at all.

ULTRA SHORT-TERM AMBITIONS

In the previous chapter, we discussed long-range ambitions, and how they can be broken down into intermediate and short-term ambitions. To explain the concept behind self management, there should be a fourth category—ultra short-term ambitions.

That's exactly what self management is. It's an ambition that a person desires to achieve within the day, week or month that feeds into a more significant ambition. When a long-range ambition is established, it's broken down into intermediate and short-term objectives. And each of those objectives is realized through ultra short-term ambitions.

For example, suppose a person unaccustomed to running sets a long-term ambition to complete a marathon. An intermediate ambition might be to run 13 miles; a short-term ambition could be completing a six-mile run. Of course, a person won't be able to achieve any of these ambitions without conditioning, which must be done over a period of time. So, for self management purposes, an ultra short-term ambition might be to run increasing distances three to four times per week. Only by following such a regimen every week can the person condition to engage successfully in long-distance running.

Of course, this same concept can be applied to any goal of any length and any type. Most worthwhile goals call for repeated action over an extended period of time. Corporate subordinates don't become chief executives overnight. They become qualified over a period of time during which they prove themselves—again and again. Writers do not create books overnight. Only by sitting down at the typewriter or word processor on a regular basis over an extended period of time do manuscripts materialize. Professional athletes, musicians and dancers aren't born great; they achieve greatness through perseverance, which results from strict practice of self management.

SHOULDERING MULTIPLE RESPONSIBILITIES

Perhaps you have several ambitions in life. Most of us do. Many of us perform in multiple roles. We are career people, parents, volunteers, church and civic leaders and, last but not least, individuals with our own desires. At one point in my life, I was a full-time high school teacher, a high school basketball coach and a part-time instructor for a well-known self-development course. Totaled, these obligations consumed 85 to 90 hours per week, and this didn't count the time involved with eating, sleeping, running errands, laundry, personal grooming and home maintenance. Although it might seem like I didn't have time to breathe, I actually found it to be a great challenge. Only through effective self management was I able to maintain this schedule without collapsing like a pup tent in a stiff wind.

If you want to perform successfully in all of your roles, it will be to your benefit to practice sound self management principles. If you already do this, then you're on your way to realizing your ambitions. If you don't, you might find getting started the toughest hill to climb. Let me show you three ways to begin practicing proper self management.

(1) **Keep a time log.** Money and time have a way of disappearing, and the person who runs out of them often can't account for all of the use. Until you know exactly where your time is going, it will be difficult to put it to better use. That is why a time log is important.

Record how you spend each quarter-hour. Discipline yourself to make an entry in your log every 15 minutes. Don't wait until the end of the day to reconstruct your actions. First, the act of reconstruction will require more time than making regular entries. And second, reconstruction defeats the purpose of the log, because, like money, people tend to forget how they use their time shortly after it's spent.

Be honest when keeping the log. If the 10-minute break stretches out to 27 minutes, make a note of it. If the one-hour lunch actually takes 99 minutes, list it. By keeping a time log for a couple of weeks, you'll come to recognize how your time is really being spent. Many people find that the 80–20 rule applies to them. This "law" states that 20% of the known variables produce 80% of the results. In the case of self management, this means that 80% of your results come from 20% of your activities. Likewise, the other 20% of your results comes from the remaining 80% of your activities. By keeping a time log, you can increase your results by focusing on the productive 20% of your activities and taking measures to practice them more often.

(2) **Maintain an activity list.** Most people would become much more efficient if they would keep an activity list. Also known as a "to do" list, it's simply a personal list of errands, commitments and responsibilities. When one pops into mind, record it on the list. That way, you can keep track of your events without fear of forgetting. Also, an activity list will make you more effective, because you won't be pausing periodically during your day to make sure you can recall all of your obligations.

Each day, review your activity list to determine which events will put you closest to realizing your ambitions. After choosing, prioritize these events. Rank them in order of importance. Then, you'll know which activities must be undertaken in which order for best results.

(3) **Devise a schedule.** A schedule is a collection of "appointments" you make. By referring to your activity list, you can assign "time slots," or specific periods of time, for activities. Some events will be easy to schedule. For example, a 10 a.m. appointment with a physician, attorney or accountant must be scheduled for 10 a.m. But obligations such as writing a report or running by the dry cleaners can be scheduled to coincide with your earliest convenience.

Keeping a schedule can help you keep in mind what is important in your life. Again, you only have 24 hours per day. If you're lucky, you'll be sleeping for six to eight of those hours. This means that you actually have 16 to 18 hours of consciousness each day to conduct your activities. When there are more events in a given day, week or month than there is time to devote to them, you'll know that the least important activities will have to be postponed or canceled.

With these three practices, you can get a good start on managing your time effectively. The log will show you where you need to improve. The activity list will show you what you need to do. And the schedule will show you when you need to do it. Together, they become powerful tools to help you use your time most effectively.

PLANNING—THE KEY TO SELF MANAGEMENT

There is nothing that will enhance your self management efforts more than planning. In their haste to save time, many people leap into a project without planning. But they generally find that a lack of planning leads to inefficient use of time.

A previous chapter pointed out that proper knowledge, skills and attitude are the three necessities for smooth performance. But when it comes to planning the execution phase of a project, there are two more phases that must be considered—time and materials. A job cannot be done without the proper tools and sufficient time to get it done.

Planning is the way to make sure all necessary items are secured before the actual execution phase begins. As a result, a great deal of time can be saved. Increasing planning time reduces execution time of a project and, as a result, decreases total time for the project. Consider the delays that might result when, in the midst of a project, you discover that vital information is missing, or that essential material is not on hand. It's generally accepted that one hour of planning saves four hours of execution.

Also, consider what happens when a two-hour task is attempted during a one-hour time frame. Either the task must be shelved until it can be completed, or whatever is scheduled for the next hour must be postponed. Without proper planning, people generally find themselves pinched for time, which means the project might be completed hurriedly—and ineffectively.

Also, planning is the step during which your activity list is compiled. Without serious planning, you'll spend your days responding to events as they materialize, rather than scheduling them to your best advantage.

So plan your days ahead of time, either first thing in the morning or during the prior evening. If you're not accustomed to planning, start small, and increase as you become more comfortable with it. Plan a half day, then work up to a whole day. Then you can tackle a week, then a month. What ambitions will you attack? What projects will you begin or end? Who will you contact? When you determine events that are urgent and plan them accordingly, you can become better aware of how much discretionary time you'll have at your disposal.

So remember the five essentials for planning—knowledge or information, skills or know-how, attitude or willingness to perform, materials and tools, and time. But perhaps most important of all is **to act.** All of the others do not amount to much unless we put action into our ambitions. Consider each of these when planning to ensure smooth execution.

SELF MANAGEMENT TIPS

Make the most of your time by practicing various time management tips that can increase your overall results. Let's examine a dozen of them.

(1) **Get organized.** If you haven't already, organize your environment. This includes your home, car and work area. Assign a space for all items, and return them to their proper places when not in use. You'll be amazed at the time you save rummaging through clutter. It is also a great psychological boost—a feeling of control and professionalism.

(2) **Handle papers once.** When documents and correspondence come to your attention, take action. Don't let them accumulate until you have a monster pile of paperwork to handle. Process papers, then file or discard them. Don't waste time shuffling them.

(3) **Ask for help when you need it.** It will take you less time to ask for and receive information than it will to conduct research or, worse yet, to learn by trial and error. Don't be too proud to ask for help when you need it. After all, you'll probably be able to return the favor in due time. This presents a strong

case for "mentors," our friends and advisors who have experienced our concerns and challenges.

(4) **"Add" productive time to your day.** There are a number of ways this can be done, including waking up earlier, going to bed later and finding ways to decrease the time devoted to successful completion of your responsibilities. Cut or eliminate breaks and lunch hours when time is of the essence.

(5) **Allow for emergencies.** When scheduling activities, don't be averse to overestimating the time required for them. This provides time for emergencies and spontaneous occurrences that require your attention. And if all goes well, the extra time can be applied to a new project or a break.

(6) **Don't "kill" short periods of time.** There are so many occasions when we can find ourselves with 10- to 20-minute blocks of time on our hands. Waiting for meetings and appointments, getting caught in traffic jams, waiting for a bus, taxi or a telephone call all qualify as "dead" time, because most people don't put them to productive use. But these time periods are dead only because we kill them. We think they are insignificant because they're of such short duration.

But do you realize that just 20 minutes a day adds up to more than 120 hours per year? That's three standard work weeks. How many books and magazine articles can you read in 120 hours? How many letters can you write in that period of time? Better yet, how much work can you do? Certainly, some work doesn't lend itself well to such small periods of time. For example, you can't write a report in 20 minutes, but you can certainly outline one. You can't tackle major projects in 20 minutes, but you can brainstorm for ideas for future ones. Keep some work, reading material and basic tools—such as paper, pencils and pocket recording devices to make notes to yourself—on hand to utilize these brief time periods. Remember, don't be afraid to think big, but don't be afraid to think small, either. By putting these seemingly insignificant periods to productive use, you can achieve significant results over the long haul.

(7) **Rely on technology.** If you're stuck in a traffic jam, you can listen to instructional cassette tape programs on a cassette recorder. Sometimes, I make my own tapes to play when I'm trying to learn new material, and I can play them while driving. Save time with a computer, microwave oven and dishwasher. When practical, use mass transportation instead of driving. You'll save not only the time involved with looking for a parking space, but you'll save parking fees, too.

(8) **Learn to say no.** Not everything you are asked to do will help you realize your ambitions. Don't be afraid to turn down requests for your assistance when compliance would interfere with the pursuit of your ambitions. Besides, it's better to refuse a request outright than to commit yourself, only to discover that you don't have enough discretionary time to honor your commitment.

(9) **Designate a daily "block time" for yourself.** Find a period of time—at least an hour—during the day when you expect minimal or no interruptions and claim that time for yourself. Use it to pursue your most important ambitions, or use it to pursue your interests. I designate 6–8 a.m. as block time, which I use for my own personal development. A friend of mine re-

serves the hour from midnight to 1 a.m., which he devotes to reading. All of us need time for ourselves. But if we don't reserve it in our schedules, we're not likely to get it.

(10) **Do it now!** W. Clement Stone popularized this concept, and it's a good one. Don't plan your work to coincide with external deadlines. If a crisis should develop, your project will be in trouble. Set your own deadlines. The more things that we make of an urgent nature, the sooner they will get done, and the better they will get done. Also, setting your own deadlines will provide an automatic "extension" should something develop to postpone the project. Procrastination can derail us from the tracks of our ambitions. It eats away at our discretionary time, and it creates "emotional baggage," or guilt over putting things off, that interferes with our effectiveness. If something is worth doing at all, it's worth doing as soon as possible.

(11) **Position yourself to discourage interruptions.** Organize a designated time when you will accept interruptions such as telephone calls or colleague visits. Keeping your office door closed will cut down on drop-in visitors. Even positioning your desk so you don't face the doorway can discourage interruptions. If people don't make eye contact with you, they'll be less inclined to intrude. Also, avoid interruptions by having someone screen your calls. Handle only the most important calls at once, and return all others during a single block of time.

(12) **Respect the time of others.** The best way to get a reputation as someone who values his or her time is by respecting other people's time. People tend to treat

individuals the same way that individuals treat them. If you respect other people's time, chances are good they'll respect yours in return.

These are only 12 tips for making the best use of time. Perhaps you can think of more. Be creative. Sales trainer Joel Weldon suggested on one of his cassette tape series checking accounts from different banks on alternating months. The benefit? He doesn't have to spend time balancing his checkbook. While he is using one, all the outstanding checks on the other are being reconciled by the bank. So each month, he receives a reconciled statement with an accurate balance.

Another good way to save time is to combine activities. Take a walk and ask a friend to join you. You get exercise and strengthen a relationship at the same time. Work during a flight. You're being productive while traveling to your destination. Listen to instructional cassette tapes while driving. You're learning while you ride. Be creative.

The key to success is good self management. Remember, long-range ambitions break down to intermediate ambitions, which break down to short-term ambitions. And those break down into ultra short-term ambitions, which is the essence of self management. By practicing good self management every day, your long-range ambitions will take care of themselves.

And the best way to maintain good self management principles is to ask yourself periodically, "Is this the most productive use of my time?" If it is, you're in good shape. If it isn't, it shouldn't be too difficult to get back on track—provided you haven't allowed yourself to stray too far.

Another way to maintain good self management habits—and all good habits, for that matter—is by choosing effective role models who have developed the habits you desire to develop yourself. The next chapter discusses the significance of role models and the importance of choosing effective ones.

CHAPTER HIGHLIGHTS

(1) Time management is impossible, but self management isn't. By decreasing the time you devote to various obligations, you can effectively increase the amount of discretionary time at your disposal.

(2) Self management is nothing more than setting and achieving ultra short-term ambitions.

(3) Practicing sound self-management principles can help you function effectively in your various life roles.

(4) The best way to get started on practicing proper self management is by keeping a time log, maintaining an activity list and devising a schedule.

(5) Increasing planning time reduces execution time of a project and, as a result, decreases total time for the project. The five essentials for planning include knowledge or information, skills or know-how, attitude or willingness to perform, materials and tools, and time.

(6) Practice various self management tips to make the best use of your time.

MY PERSONAL ACTION PLAN

** The most important idea I gained from reading this chapter is: _____

_____ .

** My plan for using this idea is: _____

_____ .

** I will commit to this idea because: _____

_____ .

** The specific actions I will take to implement this idea
are: _____

_____

_____ .

** The results I expect from my usage of this idea are: ____

_____

_____ .

Chapter Six

Mind Your Role Models

Tell me who you associate with, and I'll tell you who you are.

When I taught high school, I would say that to students. And when they identified their friends, I would identify their habits, ambitions and pastimes. It really would jolt them that someone could size them up so accurately through their association with others.

This concept is particularly interesting in the high school setting because of the different, distinguishable cliques that exist. After all, in virtually any American high school, you'll find the academic clique, the athletic clique, the alcohol clique, the drug clique, the roughnecks, the religious, the slobs, the snobs, the nerds, et al.

But doesn't the same concept apply to adults? There are so many civic clubs and organizations to accommodate people with virtually any given interest. Certainly, we can tell a lot about an individual by the company he or she keeps.

You might have heard the old warning, "If you run with dogs, you'll pick up fleas." It's a folksy way of saying, "Be careful who you associate with.'' When people associate with ''the wrong crowd,'' they likely will pick up some bad habits. And, even if they successfully resist such practices, others will judge them by their associates, anyway. It might not be right, but it's human nature.

But the same principle applies in a positive vein. When people associate with ''the right crowd,'' they are likely to assume some good habits and practices. And others will judge them by their associates, too. Again, it's just human nature.

So your friends, and especially your role models, can help make or break you.

SELECTION OF ROLE MODELS

What makes people gravitate to certain groups? Generally, people are introduced to various groups by someone they have befriended. If they like the group, they most often desire to claim affiliation with it, and be accepted by its members, to derive comfort and to feel powerful or in control. Those benefits are gained by adopting behaviors common to the group, and this most often is done by focusing on the friend who introduced them to the group. This friend becomes a role model, or a mentor, who educates subtly through demonstration. We consciously and subconsciously pattern ourselves after people we respect.

So my point is to be very careful about the role models you choose. Depending on who you admire, you can either build your strengths or build your weaknesses—if not create some new ones altogether.

Persons who are good role models don't belittle those who look up to them. They build their proteges. They allow them to share their goals, and they get excited along with them. Good role models help people climb the ladder of life that they choose; they don't try

to push them off of it. They encourage ideas and enthusiasm from
the people who look to them for guidance.

AVOID TOXIC PEOPLE

When choosing company, weed out people who would "stomp
on your dreams." People who would belittle or criticize you for
your ambitions are not friends, and they definitely should not be
your role models. The greater your ambition, the greater your need
for positive people in your life. Negative influences allowed to exist
in your environment can destroy your ambitions. Such influences
come from "toxic" people.

Toxic people tend to poison who we are and what we want to
be. They stifle our creativity and enthusiasm. They suffocate our
positive attitudes and rob us of excitement about our future. And
all this can happen without us even recognizing it.

The reason for this influence is because we tend to respect the
opinions of those we admire. We accept and adopt their attitudes
and their ways of thinking. But when we choose to admire toxic
people, we effectively place in jeopardy our attitudes and ambitions—
and all the excitement and enthusiasm that goes with them.

Some of my closest friends are people who are going up the
career ladder with me. I sincerely believe they would jump off the
ladder themselves and start all over again at the bottom before they'd
consider trying to push me down even a rung or two. Since we're
all more or less at the same point in life, they're not role models
in the strictest sense of the term.

Generally, a role model is someone with more experience and
more maturity who can serve as a guide for a younger protege.
But since my friends and I are climbing the ladder together, perhaps
we're role models for each other, holding hands, or helping each

other, on our way up. We trade ideas, share our wildest dreams and exchange encouragement and support—a perfect symbiotic relationship.

ROLE MODELS FOR EVERY OCCASION

Of course, a role model doesn't have to be affiliated with career plans. In fact, a person can have many role models, and they don't necessarily have to be older and more experienced. The late Egyptian President Anwar Sadat once said, "Whenever I see a good quality in someone else that is not in me, I always try to take it and put it in myself."

For example, my career is professional speaking. Yet, one of my role models is a young Vietnamese refugee named Dung, who speaks English with a great deal of difficulty. Certainly, she's not an effective role model in the field of communication. But when it comes to attitude, she's one of the best.

You see, Dung loves to learn, and her lack of knowledge of the English language puts her in a great position to learn something every day. She comes from a background of misery; as of this writing, her father still lives in Vietnam—as a prisoner. Her own experiences before fleeing the country were nothing to be envied. Yet, she speaks of them in terms of learning experiences, and she remembers them so she won't forget the joys of living in America—something that most of us take for granted.

It's refreshing to look at Dung and compare her attitudes with mine. After all, when I think of how she survived her anguished past, I can't help but feel a little small for letting day-to-day disappointments get me down. And, by making such a comparison, I am challenged to improve my own attitude.

Role models don't have to be human—or even real, for that

matter. I frequently clip "Garfield" cartoons to take note of Odie, the high-spirited dog who reminds me about the importance of giving and getting enough hugs and kisses, and maintaining a zest for life!

In fact, it probably wouldn't be a bad idea for humans to use dogs as behavioral role models. They don't stab each other in the back, and they most often return kindness when kindness is shown to them. Many times in encounters with humans, dogs are the first to show kindness. Perhaps we should pay more attention to dogs for some ideas about how to get along in life.

SEEK OUT THE POSITIVE

For the most part, I'm sure you'll want to stick to humans when choosing role models. Of course, I can't tell you who to choose as your role models, but I can give you some advice—stick to the positive.

Cultivate friendships with positive people. Find people who have qualities you admire and befriend them. Again, the best way to pick up any human quality is to associate with the person who possesses it.

But there are other ways this can be done. You can have a role model whom you don't know personally but with whom you are familiar through the news media. As I said in a previous chapter, basketball coach Bobby Knight is one of my role models because of his competitive spirit, inspiring personality, honesty, integrity and his individualism. As a coach, he is notorious for driving his players to become the best they are. He is vigorously opposed to bending the rules as many universities have done to build dynamic teams.

Knight builds strong teams through hard work and discipline. Academic standards he sets for his players generally are tougher than those set by the university, and he has dismissed players who didn't meet them. Here is a man who can be himself without apology.

HISTORIC ROLE MODELS

It's not even necessary for a person to be alive to be a role model. Another of my favorite role models is Harry S Truman, 33rd President of the United States. During his term in office, Truman was widely regarded as a poor president. But the nation has come to appreciate him since then for being a man who lived by his convictions and didn't mind taking a stand when it was necessary. Truman said what he thought, whether it was calling Fidel Castro a "no-good SOB" (actually, Truman used the unabbreviated version) or threatening to castrate a newspaper critic who lambasted his daughter, **Margaret Truman,** for a public vocal performance. Historians have evaluated the Truman Administration as one of great integrity and progressive in terms of bringing equality to peoples of this nation.

AND STILL MORE ROLE MODELS

Larry Bird is another role model who serves as an example of how people can overcome adversity. Reared in the small town of French Lick, Indiana, he attended one week at Indiana University before changing to a small junior college, where he lasted only two months. Back home, he got a job with the French Lick Parks Department driving a garbage truck, painting park benches and hunting mushrooms. Bird got married, but was divorced seven months later. Then his father committed suicide. This combination of tragedy and bad luck could cripple many people, but Bird instead enrolled at Indiana State University in the late 1970's and became a basketball star who gave his team true clout, scoring as many as 49 points in a single game. Now a member of the Boston Celtics, Bird is recognized as one of the top three players in the game! Coming out of ISU, many thought him to be too short and slow for the pros. But incredible hours of intense practice and a competitive spirit as to "cut your heart out" makes him what he is today.

But perhaps my biggest role model is Pete Rose, manager and former third-baseman for the Cincinnati Reds who set a record for most career hits. Known as "Charlie Hustle," Rose is the epitome of a pro. He shines with enthusiasm, sprints to first base on walks and practices hard up until the beginning of a game. Here is a man who failed one year of high school and was identified as a "non-prospect"—in other words, can't hit, throw, field or run. This man holds career records in just about every offensives category, including most hits. He has also been named to the All Star team at five different positions!

"I have to work hard to keep the edge," Rose once said. "It's hard to do that. It's hard to tell yourself you've got to go out and work your tail off in practice."

Working as hard in practice as you would for the real event is the key to success. Rose knows that, and he has earned my respect for admitting it.

But enough about my role models. They might be applicable to your situation, and, then again, they might not. The important thing is to find role models who inspire you to achieve excellence, whether it's in the realm of attitude or in your field of performance.

As James Allen said in his noted work, "As A Man Thinketh," people become what they think about. By concentrating on the admirable qualities of your role models, you can adopt these qualities and, thus, propel yourself further along your way to realizing your ambitions.

And whatever role you'd like to play in life, you can get a head start by looking the part. Appearance is a key factor in the growth of individuals whose success depends on interacting with others. And that includes just about all of us. I'll have more to say about the importance of appearance in the next chapter.

CHAPTER HIGHLIGHTS

(1) A lot can be determined about an individual by the company he or she keeps. People most often conform to the attitudes and habits of their friends and role models.

(2) Role models, or mentors, educate subtly through demonstration. We consciously and subconsciously pattern ourselves after people we respect.

(3) Good role models don't belittle those who look up to them. Good role models help people climb the ladder of life that they choose; they don't try to push them off of it.

(4) When choosing company, weed out toxic people, or those who would "stomp on your dreams." People who would belittle or criticize you for your ambitions are not friends, and they definitely should not be your role models.

(5) A role model doesn't have to be affiliated with career plans. In fact, a person can have many role models, and they don't necessarily have to be older and more experienced. When someone has a quality you'd like to possess, he or she can be a role model who can help you effect change.

(6) Cultivate friendships with positive people. Find people who have qualities you admire and befriend them. The best way to pick up any human quality is to associate with the human who possesses it.

(7) Role models can be selected from among people you know or people you know about through the media and history.

MY PERSONAL ACTION PLAN

** The most important idea I gained from reading this chapter is: _____

_____ .

** My plan for using this idea is: _____

_____ .

** I will commit to this idea because: _____

_____ .

** The specific actions I will take to implement this idea are: _____

_____

_____ .

** The results I expect from my usage of this idea are: ____

_____

_____ .

Section II

THE POWER OF PERSONAL APPEARANCE

Chapter Seven

The Value of Appearance

Given the choice between two cars of the same make and model, which would you choose—one that shone like a brand new penny or one that was dull from neglect? Speaking for myself—and probably you, too—I'd select the car that sparkled.

Salespeople know that a product's image is important to consumers, because people are attracted by a clean, crisp image. Although a given product might actually be superior to a competitor's counterpart, it might not be perceived as better if its packaging doesn't reflect its high quality.

This is not to say you can judge a product by its container. Slick packaging does not necessarily mean a product is superior. But attractive wraps virtually always command a person's attention, and that's the key issue to be discussed in this chapter.

Whether we're talking about products or people, the same rules apply. Given the choice between two salespeople with similar products, whom would you buy from—one who was dressed and groomed attractively or one who wasn't? Perhaps the poorly groomed salesperson actually sells the better product. But because of the inferior personal packaging, you might automatically favor his or her competitor, on the basis of appearance alone. These factors work on a subconscious or subliminal level of consciousness.

No, you can't judge a book by its cover. But people do, anyway. And people who don't want to be misjudged take great pains with their appearance. A sharp appearance gains positive attention that a shabby appearance doesn't rate.

Naturally, you don't have to be a salesperson to benefit from a fine appearance. People in all walks of life and in all professions will find themselves taken more seriously and better valued by their peers if they display a sharp appearance. To get ahead, we must package ourselves as important products, because everyone is in the business of selling something. Either we sell products, our advice or our credibility. If we want people to buy, we'd better look the part.

A FINE LINE BETWEEN SELF-IMAGE AND APPEARANCE

Although there are exceptions to every rule, people who have healthy self-images most often take the greatest pride in their appearance. People with poor self-images don't value themselves and, thus, usually don't take efforts to present themselves in the most favorable light.

When I taught an evening personal development course, one of my students was a young woman named Jane who enrolled at the urging of her employer. Jane's boss had warned that I was going to have my work cut out in trying to encourage this woman to develop herself. The employer said Jane operated from a negative attitude. She could not do her job satisfactorily, and she was negative.

The Value of Appearance

She was grossly overweight and negative. Her appearance was awful, and she was negative. Negative, negative, negative!

The first night I met Jane, I realized that her boss had absolutely underestimated her negativeness. She came into the classroom looking like she wanted to kill—which I imagine she did. After all, it usually takes a certain amount of positive attitude to enroll in a self-development course, and Jane didn't even have that. I suspect that she enrolled only because her employer made it a condition of continued employment.

Jane's negative facial expressions were in perfect harmony with the rest of her body. In addition to being overweight, she was notoriously unkempt. Her hair looked like it hadn't been washed in days. Her clothes were wrinkled and of extremely poor quality.

But she attended the course sessions and paid particular attention when we discussed self-image, self-esteem and self-confidence. And I believe she started to work out her own problems, because after a couple of weeks, she began to smile—something she hadn't done previously.

Jane began to see herself in a different, more positive light. As the course progressed, she started to talk more and interact positively with others. She became a little more outgoing. Her hygiene was improving, and I noticed she was starting to wear new, brighter and better-quality clothing.

I think Jane is a prime example of how self-image and personal appearance are entwined. In fact, they are so closely connected that something that impacts one will affect the other—either positively or negatively. For example, when people let their appearance slide, they often become down on themselves. And the reverse is true. When people are down on themselves, they often let their appearance slide. Think of your feelings on a rainy Monday morning. Our attitude may be down and we prepare ourselves accordingly. So it's easy to see how the relationship between self-image and personal appearance can amount to a vicious cycle. When one suffers, so does the other, which generates even more suffering, ad nauseum. The personal damage continues to mount.

But the cycle also applies positively. When people feel good about themselves, they tend to take good physical care of themselves through exercise and good grooming. As they reap the benefits of good personal care, they feel better about themselves, which makes them take better care of themselves, ad infinitum. That's what is called a loving cycle, because the benefits get better the longer the cycle is perpetuated.

Self-image and personal appearance feed off each other. Whether the mutual feeding is nourishing or destructive depends on how you feel about yourself and how much care you take with your appearance. People who take good care of both will be better able to move out of their comfort zones, strike new friendships and explore new career possibilities. They'll feel more confident about themselves and their abilities.

Now, what about Jane? Did she shed all of her excess weight and become the most sought-after date in town? All I can say is that she was well on her way by the end of the course. At that point, she had gained the admiration and respect of her peers. That was quite an accomplishment for a woman who originally couldn't bring herself to smile. And if she continues to develop a positive self-image, there's no telling where life might take her.

SNAP DECISIONS?

Psychologists say that people make up their minds about us within the first four to 10 seconds after meeting us. And within the first five minutes of interaction, people have a total picture of who we are, based on how we have presented ourselves in terms of our actions, attitudes and appearance.

These decisions often are made subliminally. For example, if we're standing in a supermarket checkout line, we might look at the shopper ahead and notice the items he or she intends to purchase.

If the shopper is disheveled and overweight and pushing a buggy loaded down with cookies, pastries, soft drinks, ice cream and other high-calorie foods, we might form the impression that the shopper is a slob whose prime interest in life is achieving oral gratification.

On the other hand, if the shopper is neat and trim and is purchasing healthy foods, we might form the impression that the individual has a high self-image and is interested in maintaining good physical health. We might deduce that a shopper whose cart is filled with beer, wine and potato chips is a "party animal," while another shopper who is buying a dozen steaks and a huge bag of charcoal might be planning a cookout.

Of course, these deductions are more or less evident. But it's interesting to consider other images that come to mind when observing people at the supermarket. Judging by the way they dress and talk and by what they buy, we can form images about where they live, their socio-economic background, their work status (blue or white collar), whether they live alone or with others and, above all, whether we'd like to get to know them better. Of course, some of these images might lend themselves to incorrect impressions. But, in the real world, people judge others by these images. So it's vital to your success that you go out of your way to create the type of image you want others to receive.

GLOW FROM THE INSIDE OUT

Have you ever noticed how some people seem to shine? They seem to possess a natural radiance that "glows." And, to some extent, they do glow. A fine personal appearance can be described as both an inner glow and an outer glow. Both must be present to create the total image. Let's examine what each is.

(1) **Inner glow.** This comes from the self-image, a personal understanding of who we are and what we're able to

do. All the grooming and fine clothes in the world won't hold attention like the inner glow can. As we discovered with Jane, a person's self-image is reflected in his or her posture (erect or slumped), facial expressions (smile or frown), eye contact (or lack of it), handshake (firm or limp) and our voice (strong or weak, friendly or distant).

(2) **Outer glow.** These are the external factors of our appearance, including clothing, personal hygiene, condition of hair, skin and nails, vitality and manners—all of which we'll discuss in detail in future chapters. Care devoted to these externals creates an outer glow. Such care shows that we feel good about ourselves and that we're proud of who we are.

You might have heard of the expression, "Who you are speaks so loudly, I can't hear what you're saying." Obviously, this means that a person can talk all day about how talented or skilled he or she might be. But if the appearance isn't congruent with a successful image, no one is likely to buy it.

On the other hand, you also might have heard of the "halo effect." This is when a person makes such a fine first impression that people think he or she can do no wrong. When people are sufficiently impressed with a new person, they become "sold," sometimes even going so far as to make concessions for the person's mistakes.

I reaped the benefit of the "halo effect" when I called on a major business in greater Harrisburg, Pennsylvania. Although the business had an excellent training department, I attempted to sell my services as a trainer. I could have been very intimidated by the company trainers who interviewed me. After all, they could have written me off as "just another speaker" looking for a job.

I spent a couple of hours discussing ideas. Of course, I had to know my material, but my appearance was the key to getting the interview and maintaining my confidence. As a result, it made a good impression on the trainers, who hired me.

Self-image and good grooming is essential to making a fine first impression. But so is tasteful clothing. I'll explain why in the next chapter.

CHAPTER HIGHLIGHTS

(1) A clean, crisp image is vital to the person who would make a fine first impression. People in all walks of life and all professions will find themselves taken more seriously and valued more highly by their peers if they display a sharp appearance.

(2) To get ahead, we must package ourselves as important products, because everyone is in the business of selling something. Either we sell products, our advice or our credibility. If we want people to buy, we'd better look the part.

(3) Self-image and personal appearance are so closely connected that impact on one will have its effects on the other—either positive or negative.

(4) Psychologists say that people make up their minds about us within the first four to 10 seconds after meeting us. And within the first five minutes of interaction, people have a total picture of who we are, based on how we have presented ourselves in terms of our actions, attitudes and appearance.

(5) First impressions are powerful, because people generally form lasting opinions of us on that basis. And making a good first impression is extremely critical to a budding relationship, because it's one of the few things in life at which you won't get a second chance.

(6) Appearance has nothing to do directly with a person's talents and skills, but it has everything to do with gaining another person's attention. Without attention, people will have a difficult time proving themselves.

(7) A fine appearance consists of an inner glow, which results from a positive self-image, and an outer glow, which including clothing, hygiene, condition of hair, skin and nails, vitality and manners.

(8) When a person makes a good first impression, he or she usually creates the "halo effect," which means that others will be "sold" on him or her.

MY PERSONAL ACTION PLAN

** The most important idea I gained from reading this chapter is: _____

_____.

** My plan for using this idea is: _____

_____.

** I will commit to this idea because: _____

_____.

The Value of Appearance

**   The specific actions I will take to implement this idea are: _____

_____

_____ .

**   The results I expect from my usage of this idea are: ____

_____

_____ .

Chapter Eight

Clothing Catches the Eye

Think clothes do not make a difference? How would you react if yours were to disappear suddenly?

All jokes aside, our clothes have quite an impact on others, especially when they first meet us. After all, 90% of a first impression is appearance, and since up to 90% of our bodies is covered with clothes, it's evident that your choice of clothes plays a large part in the image you create with others.

There is a Harvard University study that backs this up. Essentially, it states that the way we dress influences the way we feel about ourselves, which influences the way we behave. Naturally, the way we behave influences the way others will respond to us. So, the logical conclusion is that clothing is a major influence on the way others respond to us.

I believe this study is right on the money. After all, who doesn't take note of the presence of a uniformed police officer. Plainclothes police don't create the same image as those whose outfits announce to the public that they are armed enforcers of the law. Likewise, firefighters wear uniforms that command respect. If you were watching a house burn and realized you were in the path of a uniformed firefighter, you'd likely step aside. If the firefighter were wearing regular street clothes, you might not be able to distinguish between him or her and an average citizen.

But consider the impact uniforms have on police officers and firefighters. They aren't directly affected by their clothing. They could arrest criminals and fight fires in blue jeans. Yet, the respect their uniforms command from others will build their self-image in their occupational roles.

WE ALL WEAR "ON-THE-JOB" UNIFORMS

Most people follow some type of spoken or unspoken dress codes at their places of employment. As a result, we all wear uniforms of sorts. Mechanics, cooks, sanitation engineers, mail carriers, milk deliverers, airplane pilots and airline attendants all wear uniforms. So do business executives.

True, executives' outfits do not always follow a common cut and style as formal uniforms do. But executives wear uniforms, just the same, in that they're expected to create a certain image. And the image such informal uniforms create depends largely on their quality.

I have discovered that this is true from first-hand experiences. There is a fine restaurant in the Washington DC area I have visited several times, and it seems the quality of my treatment each time has been directly connected with the way I was dressed. Certainly, this is no scientific study, but I feel that it's happened too many times for it to be coincidental.

On one of my first visits there, I was wearing what is commonly called a "power outfit"—a finely tailored navy blue suit, a crisp white shirt and a silk tie to compliment the ensemble. The treatment I received that evening was superb. The restaurant's staff went out of their way to create a wonderful evening for my guest and me.

On a subsequent visit, I was clad in a sport coat and slacks. While there was nothing wrong with the outfit, it seemed to suggest more of a relaxed or youthful appearance than my power outfit. And—I believe as a result of my dress—it was amazing the difficulties I experienced. I was hit in the head with a tray—twice—and a fork was dropped in my lap. The offending staff members apologized, but I did not sense that their apologies were sincere. On top of that, my guest and I were more or less rushed through our meals. Overall, it was not an enjoyable evening.

Granted, it could have been coincidence. But as I pointed out, I had similar experiences later—both positive and negative—at the same restaurant. As a rule, I was treated well when I was clad in impressive clothes. But when I wore something less than impressive, I was just another order blank to the restaurant.

CLOTHES SET THE STAGE FOR INTERACTION

So these experiences and others helped me realize that there are three assumptions we can make when meeting others, based solely on their clothing. Let's examine them.

(1) **You are more important than me.** Remember, we're just talking about an assumption, not a reality. Certainly, a corporate chairman might be extremely important to the organization, but he or she might not have any real significance outside headquarters. However, the person who meets the CEO might assume otherwise because of his or her fine clothing.

(2) **You are my equal.** In the military, the stripes of rank determine how people react to each other. In life, it's the quality and style of clothing. When two people are dressed in clothes with more or less the same style and quality, they often accept each other as equals in terms of socio-economic standing.

(3) **You are not as important as I am.** It might seem snobbish, but it's human nature. How do you know a bum when you see one? Unless you know the bum personally, you can only judge by appearance, which depends mostly on clothing. When we see someone with mismatched clothing of poor quality, we draw conclusions—right or wrong. If the person were to approach us, we might react coldly because we'd think he or she was asking for a handout.

Again, these assumptions are subjective by nature and aren't necessarily correct. But appearance creates impressions, and clothes create appearance. Back in the 1960's, if you wanted to be branded as a "hippie" or a "freak," all that was necessary was to wear faded blue jeans with patches, an old flannel shirt and a peace medallion. Of course, even the "hippies" came to realize the significance of conformity. As they aged, most of them shed their "uniforms" for more socially acceptable clothing.

DRESS FOR YOUR DREAMS

And that brings to mind an important point about dress. When selecting clothes, we should not dress for who we are, but for who we aspire to be. I do not mean that we should be pretentious, nor am I suggesting that we overdress beyond the point of practicality.

A construction worker who clocks in wearing a suit might get some strange looks. Also, the worker will not be as effective on the job because a suit just isn't practical for construction work.

By dressing for the role you would like to assume, you do two things. First, of course, you create the image of a competent professional with both management and your clients. Second, you create the self-image of a competent and able person worthy of promotion. And while clothes won't improve your performance directly, remember the Harvard study—a fine choice of clothes makes us feel better about ourselves, which improves our self-image. And, of course, an improved self-image will lead to improved performance.

All things considered, good clothing isn't a bad investment, is it?

CLOTHES MAKE THE PERSON

Of course, clothes can't make us look like something we're not. We can't regulate genetics, but we can accentuate our positive features and control the way we present our undesirable aspects.

For example, pleated trousers can help conceal excess abdominal weight. Vertical stripes can make a large person appear thinner, while horizontal stripes can make a smaller person appear broader. Certain colors like navy blue can create a powerful appearance— especially for a shorter person.

When choosing clothing, ask yourself the following questions:

(1) **Considering my job and the company for which I work, is this appropriate for me to wear?** This is the first consideration. Many people invest more money in special occasion clothing than they do in the clothes that they wear for work. Certainly, since most of your waking hours are spent at your job, most of your clothes

should be appropriate for the workplace. A hairstylist or rock musician would want to wear trendy or faddish styles to communicate with their "with-itnesses," while a banker, being entrusted with people's hard-earned dollars, would want to communicate a more conservative message.

(2) **Is it good basic fashion or faddish?** This is an important question. For the most part, fads have no place on the job. The basic clothing code for business is to dress to please your most conservative client of the day. The reason being that a liberal client will forgive you for dressing conservatively much quicker than a conservative client will make concessions for fads that he or she might view as inappropriate. Also, fads are like light bulbs; they burn bright and hot for a relatively short period of time, then they're junk.

(3) **Is it a good style for my body size and shape?** Remember, a garment that looks good on one person might not be at all complimentary to another. One reason clothes come in various cuts and styles is because bodies come in various sizes and shapes.

(4) **Does it fit properly?** There is nothing that can give a second-rate look as much as ill-fitting clothes. Trouser legs that rise significantly above shoe-top level scream for replacement. So do extremely tight sweaters and jackets for both women and men. By the same token, oversized clothing can make you look more like Charlie Chaplin than what you aspire to be. Make sure your clothing fits well.

(5) **Is it right for this situation?** If you call on top management of Fortune 500 companies, you'd better not look like a slouch. But, equally as important, it's not smart to overdress for other situations. For example, if you're

trying to sell a cash register to the proprietor of a short-order diner, a fine suit might not be the best outfit. If the proprietor is clad in an apron and paper hat, he or she might be intimidated out of buying.

Also, it's important to consider the area of the country in which you operate. Wool suits and heavy shoes are appropriate in the northeast, where winter weather can be harsh. In the south, suits and shoes of lighter material will suffice. Bright colors are more acceptable on the west coast than in other parts of the country. And southwest businessmen often wear cowboy boots with three-piece suits. That's perfectly fine, as long as they don't plan to leave the region.

(6) **Are the fabric and cut of top quality so that your garment will be an investment?** Buying top quality might cost more, but it will last longer, which means you'll get more value out of it. For example, let's say a $500 suit will last five years. If you wear it once a week, it would cost you only about $2 each time. That's not a bad investment at all. Also, consider the impression that top quality will help create. If your success depends on impressing others, go first-class. Spend twice as much and buy half as many items. When you consider how much potential income you can lose through making the wrong impression, you'll realize you simply cannot afford to go any other way than first class.

(7) **Will this project me as successful, self-confident and competent?** Again, clothes might have no direct bearing on our ability. We have to prove that ourselves. But whether we get the chance to prove ourselves depends on how good an impression we make.

Of course, clothes are not the sole determining factor of image. Professional behavior and competency still count in this society, thank goodness. But clothing is certainly the outer component of image. Packaging ourselves as important products calls for fine presentation of our exteriors, and clothes count in that department.

WHAT COLOR IS SUCCESS?

The proper fit and style are only two points of the triangle when choosing an appropriate suit. The third point is color. Of course, choosing the appropriate color is a subjective process that often depends on the build of the wearer. Let's take a look at popular opinions when it comes to color selection in clothing.

(1)   **Navy blue.** This is the ultimate in power suits, although some people feel that large men and women should avoid it because it makes them appear too overbearing.

(2)   **Dark grey.** According to clothing experts, small persons should avoid this color. Otherwise, it's a safe choice to wear in virtually any business situation.

(3)   **Medium blue.** A safe color for any business occasion and any sized person. The color connotes an air of authority combined with an image of being approachable. This is a fine color for a leader.

(4)   **Light grey.** Good for tall people—especially those who are strong on giving orders. The lighter the shade, the more approachable a person generally appears.

(5)   **Light blue.** Although this color works well on tall people and people with strong personalities, great care should be used in selecting it. There are so many shades of light blue that choosing the wrong one for your situation is likely. Unless you're absolutely sure it's for you, find another color.

(6) **Medium grey.** This color is safe with all except heavy individuals. It's a positive for strong personalities and doesn't detract from people who aren't good at giving orders.

And, of course, don't forget accessories for the finishing touches. The image a fine suit creates can be negated with the wrong shirt and tie. Scuffed and inappropriate shoes also can ruin an otherwise fine first impression. Jewelry should always be tasteful. "Skin-diver" wrist watches should be avoided by both sexes. As a rule, the less jewelry, the better, although women can get by with wearing more than men.

There are all types of "rules" on clothing. But perhaps the best rule is never to let an expert's rule override your common sense. You are a unique individual who will look good in some colors and styles, while others won't do you justice. Unless you are extremely secure with your personal tastes in clothes, I would suggest dealing with a store and clerk you have developed a good relationship with and have experienced success with past purchases. It's also not a bad idea to take along a friend who knows and understands your business for a second opinion when shopping.

Appearance is important, and clothes are important to appearance. But so is good hygiene and health. Even if your suit is fit for royalty, what kind of an impression will you make if you—yourself—look like death warmed over. Check out the next chapter for tips on how to make yourself shine, regardless of what you might be wearing.

CHAPTER HIGHLIGHTS

(1) The way we dress influences the way we feel about ourselves, which influences the way we behave. Naturally,

the way we behave influences the way others will respond to us. So, the logical conclusion is that clothing has a major influence on the way others respond to us.

(2) Most people follow some type of spoken or unspoken dress codes at their places of employment. As a result, we all wear uniforms of sorts.

(3) Clothes set the stage for interaction. A person can be perceived as inferior, equal or superior to another on the basis of attire.

(4) When selecting clothes, we shouldn't dress for who we are, but for who we aspire to be. This creates an image of competency, both with others and yourself.

(5) When choosing clothes, be sure they're appropriate for your business, fashionable but not faddish, congruent with your body size and shape, properly fitted, right for your particular situation, of top quality and congruent with a good image.

(6) Colors are subjective decisions. While there are some guidelines that can be followed, try to deal with a clerk whose tastes you trust, and for additional opinion take along a friend.

MY PERSONAL ACTION PLAN

** The most important idea I gained from reading this chapter is: _____

_____ .

** My plan for using this idea is: _____

_____ .

** I will commit to this idea because: _____

_____ .

** The specific actions I will take to implement this idea
are: _____

_____

_____ .

** The results I expect from my usage of this idea are: ____

_____

_____ .

Chapter Nine

Health Habits Plus Hygiene Yield Energy

Would it be important to you to lose 20 pounds, gain more energy and function effectively with only five hours of sleep? Would you like to be able to work 60 to 85 hours per week—working from 7:30 a.m. to midnight, full of excitement and enthusiasm—and still enjoy good health?

This lifestyle can be yours—if it isn't already—if you're willing to eat a balanced diet, eat it at proper times, exercise, and avoid excesses.

Maintaining good health is critical to presenting your best appearance. While clothes can accentuate and control our physical appearances to some extent, neither clothes nor cosmetics will make a person appear healthy if he or she really is not.

When presenting our best image, it is important to take steps beyond proper clothes selection. Although clothes play a large part in making a first impression, they do not do the entire job. People will be looking at our faces and hands, and our bodies in general. To make a fine first impression, it's important that we make ourselves as appealing as possible. Good health and good grooming are the keys.

EAT RIGHT—AND AT THE RIGHT TIMES

Eating a balanced diet isn't enough for good health. I have found that it's not only important what I eat, but when I eat it. For three years, I have followed a very interesting diet regimen that has helped me avoid major colds and viruses.

Starting in the mornings, I eat only fruits. This gives me a great deal of energy through the day. As for lunch and supper, I continue with fruits and vegetables—foods high in water content—occasionally enjoying lean chicken or fish. I try to avoid red meats during the week because they sometimes make me feel sluggish. Red meats are higher in fat, calories and cholesterol.

But this is not to say that I don't like red meat, because I do. And, on the weekends when I'm not working, I'll eat cheesesteaks, pizza, donuts, cookies and ice cream. Just knowing I can reward myself on the weekends helps me hold the course during the week. By choosing what foods to eat and when, I can function at my optimum level.

Also, I try not to eat anything after 9 p.m. If I must have something, I'll have fruit or popcorn cooked in olive oil—no salt or butter. The purpose for not eating late at night is so my body won't be digesting food and using energy while I sleep.

As for exercise, it helps me work into the evenings. After putting in a full day, I'll go out to run or attend aerobics class at a local health club. Exercise is best in late afternoon or early evening because the body's metabolism is winding down. At that point, exercise can "stoke the fire" to increase it, building energy and making it easier to be enthusiastic about continuing with the day. And I find that I can get some quality work completed in the evening hours. Also, exercise helps me control my weight.

Now I do take breaks, and I try to work in an afternoon rest period of about 15 to 30 minutes. I have found that if I can get that much "quiet time" in the afternoon, it can add an hour or two onto my evenings. At a convenient time, somewhere between 3:30–5:30 p.m., if I can just lie down on a sofa, a bed or even my desk for 15 to 30 minutes with my eyes closed, I will soon feel very refreshed and well rested. I am not suggesting sleep, but rather a "quiet time" to replenish my systems.

THE PRIZE FOR THE PRICE

I'm no masochist. I wouldn't subject myself to this lifestyle if I didn't enjoy it. So let me discuss the benefits. Since I've followed this regimen, the worst illness I get is a slight cold that may last about three or four days. I don't suffer from depression or the aches and pains that accompany major colds and the flu.

I have lost between 20 and 30 pounds that I needed to lose, and I feel significantly more energetic than before. I work 60 to 85 hours per week, and fatigue is rarely a problem. Normally, I sleep only four to six hours per night. On weekends when I'm not busy, I do sleep a little more. But if I have a trip planned, my standard four to six hours will get me through just fine.

Good health is important for so many reasons. Of course, it prolongs life. No elaboration needed here. But subliminally—although not necessarily of lesser importance—is the fact that good health and a trim physique is a positive influence on a person's self-image. The better we look and feel, the better we feel about ourselves. As a result, we will perform better, and others will respond to us more positively.

BE CONSISTENT WITH SLEEP

Although I can get by with only four to six hours of sleep per night, I know many people who need the standard seven to eight. Of course, there's nothing wrong with this. People have different needs.

But I've learned there are some ways to reduce the amount of sleep you need and guard against waking up feeling drained.

(1) **Stay in shape.** The person who takes the time to exercise vigorously three times per week probably can regain that time investment by reducing sleep. The body functions more efficiently when it gets proper exercise. Oxygen flow to the bloodstream is increased, muscles are toned and the amount of fat is reduced. Together, these benefits eliminate some of the body's need for rest.

(2) **Avoid eating before bedtime.** People who make it a habit to have a "midnight snack" before retiring aren't doing themselves any favors. As we've already seen, the body that must digest food while it sleeps is using energy that will likely be missed in the morning.

(3) **Go to bed at the same time each night.** This is where many people run into trouble. They'll go to bed at 11 p.m. one night, 1 a.m. the next. With no set bedtime, their body has no set schedule. A consistent bedtime is the key to setting a good sleep schedule. The body functions best when it gets the same amount of rest every day.

It's better to get less sleep and remain consistent than to get irregular amounts of sleep. Don't tax the body by being inconsistent. If I am traveling, I keep my watch set on Eastern time and will follow Eastern time throughout my stay.

EXERCISE, DON'T JUST DIET

If excess fat is standing in the way of physical fitness, then it's obviously got to go. But there is a right way and a wrong way to do it.

The right way is through maintaining a proper diet and exercising sufficiently to burn up more calories than you take in. The wrong way is through "crash" or "fad" dieting, or depriving your body of a significant portion of its accustomed caloric intake.

Let me explain why the wrong way doesn't work. The body has the ability to accommodate changing conditions. When it's cold, we shiver to generate warmth; when it's hot, we perspire to release body heat and fluids. When we starve ourselves, the body compensates by lowering its metabolism, which means that fewer calories will be burned. So the longer a person diets, the fewer calories the body will burn. For the most part, any pounds lost will be limited to water weight and muscle—precisely the type of weight you don't want to lose. And, when the person drops the diet and resumes old eating habits, even more fat will be gained because the body is operating under a lower metabolic rate, and burning fewer calories, than before. Fad diets **always** include a decrease of caloric intake. And they deny certain essential foods or increase one or more foods.

Now, let's talk about the right way. By changing eating habits, or maintaining a proper diet, the body will become accustomed to a lower level of caloric intake. But regular exercise will keep the metabolic rate at a level high enough to burn calories, which means the body will lose fat.

Losing weight and keeping it off often takes a long time. But the longer you take, the less painful the process will be. Cutting back just 100 calories per day can make the difference of more than 10 pounds within a year. Unfortunately, most people don't pace themselves. They start out "gung-ho" and burn out when results don't rapidly materialize.

If you have more weight than you'd like, just remember that it didn't get there overnight, and it won't go away overnight, either. Exercise, revise your eating habits and look at the venture as a long-term effort. Visualize yourself as being in shape, and allow your self-image to improve with the size of your body. In time, your efforts will be rewarded.

MODERATION, NOT EXCESSES

Many people would enjoy good health and fitness, were it not for their excesses. There are several common "vices" that can interfere with good health when taken to extremes. Let's examine them.

(1) **Nicotine.** The U.S. government now says this drug is as addictive as cocaine and heroin. Almost anyone who has ever dropped the addiction will tell you its tough. Health experts say this is one vice people should avoid altogether. If you're hooked and don't want to give it up, at least try to cut down.

(2) **Alcohol.** According to some medical experts, this agent isn't all bad. Two beers, glasses of wine or shots of whiskey per day supposedly will add years to your life by softening your arteries and breaking down life-threatening cholesterol deposits near the heart. How-

ever, anything more than two drinks per day becomes counterproductive and harmful. Alcohol also can interfere with your sleep. Although you might become drowsy after a nightcap, the alcohol detracts from the quality of your sleep, and might even cause you to wake up during the night.

(3) **Caffeine.** Like nicotine, it's a perfectly legal drug. And, like nicotine, it can offer adverse effects when taken in large doses. Too much caffeine can cause nervousness, heart palpitations and anxiety. Too much of it over the years can lead to poor health. Keep caffeine consumption down for best health.

(4) **Drugs.** This is a wide topic, ranging from prescribed tranquilizers to illegal drugs such as cocaine and marijuana. Prescribed or not, the body will function best without mind-altering agents. If you currently are taking prescribed tranquilizers, why not talk to your physician about weaning yourself off?

(5) **Food.** Of course, we need food to live—to a point. Past that point, it interferes with the quality of our lives through excess weight and poor health. Exercise can help decrease your appetite. So can drinking a glass of water before mealtimes. Eating slowly also can help, thus allowing time for your stomach to fill. Too many people wolf down more food than their stomachs can accommodate, thus leading to excess weight gain—and post-mealtime stomach cramps.

(6) **Sweets.** People with otherwise good health habits can ruin their health if they have a compulsion for sweets. I'd be the last person to tell you to quit these. But I'll be the first to tell you that you'll come to appreciate them more through moderation.

It's a rare person who doesn't have a penchant for at least one of these potential excesses. If one or more is threatening your health, I'd urge you to eliminate it. Seek professional help if necessary. And make sure other problems don't rise to threaten you later by partaking of any potential health threat in moderation.

PRACTICE GOOD GROOMING

Hygiene is a critical factor toward maintaining good health and sufficient energy. It's not that good hygiene gives us energy, but the lack of it can certainly make us feel drained. After all, don't you feel much better in the morning as you step out of the shower than you did stepping in?

Naturally, hygiene is vital to presenting your best appearance. The finest clothes money can buy won't help your image if your personal hygiene leaves much to be desired. Let's examine the four points of good hygiene.

(1) **Skin.** Baths or showers take care of this department. Aside from keeping it clean, regular bathing helps keep pores opened, which makes for better looking skin. Regular exercise also can help improve the condition of your skin, because the body will perspire and eliminate many impurities.

I also suggest a regimen of gentle facial cleansers that will cleanse gently without drying. Toners remove impurities and close pores. Moisturizers maintain a soft and youthful glow. Monthly facials will cleanse deeply into the pores and provide much needed circulation of blood.

(2) **Hair:** Clean, neatly styled hair is critical to making a fine first impression. The face generally is the first thing

we notice about a person, which means his or her hair gets our attention, too. A survey of executives disclosed that hair is one of the first things observed in overall appearance—specifically, proper style and neatness.

(3) **Nails.** Unkempt fingernails can ruin an otherwise fine first impression. Keep them tastefully trimmed and cleaned. If you're in the habit of biting them, try chewing gum instead. Bitten nails indicate that you are not serious about appearance. I have regularly scheduled manicures. As an image consultant, I must be my best self at all times.

(4) **Teeth.** Most bad breath results from poor dental care. Regular brushing and flossing not only keeps your mouth and teeth clean and fresh, but it also helps avoid the build-up of plaque, which can lead to gum disease and, if left untreated, loss of teeth.

When you think about it, making a fine first impression is quite a responsibility. It requires taking care of your body so you can present your best appearance. And, as we've seen, taking care of yourself is an all-day job. It calls for the continual practice of good health and hygiene habits.

But there's still more to making a fine first impression. So let's move on to the next chapter, where we'll discuss the power of body language and how important it is to make sure your non-verbal expressions are congruent with what you intend to communicate. It's an essential part of making a fine first impression.

CHAPTER HIGHLIGHTS

(1) Maintaining good health is critical to presenting your best appearance. While clothes can accentuate and control our

physical appearances to some extent, neither clothes nor cosmetics will make a person appear healthy if he or she really is not.

(2) Eating a balanced diet at the proper times is essential for good health and maximum energy.

(3) Some ways to reduce the amount of sleep you need and guard against waking up feeling drained include staying in shape, avoiding eating before bedtime and following a consistent bedtime.

(4) The best way to lose fat and keep it off is through a combination of exercising and maintaining a proper diet. "Crash" or "fad" diets usually fail.

(5) Consume potential excesses in moderation to avoid long-term health problems.

(6) Hygiene is a critical factor for maintaining good health and sufficient energy.

MY PERSONAL ACTION PLAN

** The most important idea I gained from reading this chapter is: _____

_____ .

** My plan for using this idea is: _____

_____ .

Health Habits Plus Hygiene Yield Energy

** I will commit to this idea because: _____

_____ .

** The specific actions I will take to implement this idea
are: _____

_____

_____ .

** The results I expect from my usage of this idea are: ___

_____

_____ .

Chapter Ten

The "Talking" Body

Sometimes, people's words don't tell the whole story. They might say they understand or are in agreement with you. Yet, something about them tells you that they're not telling the truth. Something is causing you to have doubts.

Actually, that "something" that tells you all is not as it appears to be is their body language, which is a broad category encompassing everything from posture to facial expressions. And make no mistake, body language is a stronger form of communication than is the spoken word.

According to communication expert B.F. Skinner, 70% to 80% of all communication is non-verbal. That might be hard to believe, but think about it. How do we know when people like us? Often, it's not because they tell us so. It may be because of their facial expressions and body positioning when we're near them. As Skinner said, we're all products of our environments, and we're going to react to those environments. This is often done without thinking.

People's bodies and facial expressions most often tend to reflect their emotions. A lone pedestrian who encounters a menacing street gang very likely will react in a manner that will reflect emotion—in this case, possible fear and anxiety. Likewise, if he or she met an old friend, the same pedestrian's reaction would be much different. But the reaction still would reflect emotions and, as a result, might communicate the feeling to the other person or group.

Our words are meant to convey our thoughts, but people look at our faces and bodies for the real story. If our facial expressions and postures are congruent with our words, then we've communicated effectively. If they aren't, our listeners might not believe us—and rightly so.

So it's a good idea to remember that our facial and bodily expressions play a major role in communication. The way we present our facial expressions and postures is a vital portion of the way we package ourselves. To make a fine first impression, it's important to be sure our facial and bodily expressions agree with our thoughts.

CONFLICTING SIGNALS

During my high school teaching career, I often conducted a brief experiment to illustrate the power of body language. Teenagers aren't always aware of its significance. But rather than try to explain it to them, I'd show them—using the students as subjects for the experiment.

As a teacher, students were forever approaching me on the basis of some need. When I would conduct this experiment, I would demonstrate how negative body language could be discouraging. When they would talk, I would turn away my head, fold my arms, cross my legs or even talk to another student. I would use every rude and inappropriate body stance that came to mind.

Of course, this was just an experiment to generate an impression.

122

And, in most cases, I was successful. The students weren't pleased. They drew the impression that I wasn't interested in what they had to say. They became inhibited in their conversation, and many times didn't even finish their questions. Then I would explain how important body language is to the communication process. I would illustrate this by having them repeat their messages, to which I would then respond by displaying an attentive posture. As a result, the students felt more confident and more open in sharing their thoughts. (This was an effective lesson for demonstrating how we can enhance our relationships with others.)

Let's examine some common non-verbal communication skills to give you an idea of the significance of body language.

(1) **Eye contact.** Unless two people are engaged in a Mexican standoff, eye contact generally is a positive sign of interaction. Inability to make eye contact signifies disinterest, discomfort or resentment.

(2) **Nodding approval.** When combined with eye contact and smiles, nodding approval is a strong sign of understanding and agreement. But standing alone, nodding approval can be a listener's way of indicating that he or she is anxious for you to stop talking.

(3) **Smiling.** An honest smile indicates interest, acceptance and approval. Unfortunately, all smiles aren't sincere, and it doesn't usually take an expert to determine whether any given smile is genuine or superficial.

(4) **Touching.** This is a strong sign of approval and acceptance that can be extremely constructive when accompanied by positive actions. But touching can be an extremely destructive force when used to reproach. Again, it doesn't take an expert to tell the difference. You must be very careful. Some people do not care to touch, nor enjoy being touched. They may take offense.

(5) **Handshakes.** A handshake reveals so much about a person. When two people clasp each others' hands firmly, each are indicating they are glad to meet or see the other. Done improperly, it can harm an otherwise fine first impression. A "dead fish" handshake does not leave me with a valued impression, and I don't think I'm in a minority in that view.

These are just some of the more common modes of nonverbal communication. But bodily communication can be more sophisticated.

KEEPING DISTANCE

If you've ever been cornered by a crusader at an airport or a bus terminal, you probably felt some degree of discomfort. Aside from the fact that the individual was looking for a handout, your discomfort might have been caused by the person's violating your personal space.

Personal space is an area of about two feet that individuals more or less stake out for themselves, unless circumstances don't permit.

For example, people in a crowded elevator, subway or bus often must forego any personal space to accommodate others. But in normal situations, the 24 inches extending around a person is reserved for him or her, loved ones and close friends.

When strangers, mere acquaintances or people we don't like violate our personal space, we become threatened and resentful. Such an intrusion most often is perceived as an act of aggression, and the offended individual usually rejects messages from such intruders.

As a rule, strangers should remain at least six feet apart. Acquaintances, co-workers and clients can safely move within the two- to six-feet range of each other—unless they have established friendly relations, in which case they might feel comfortable even closer.

Be careful when you move into someone's personal space. If you're not welcome, you can actually impede good communication. And never move into someone's personal space on first meeting— unless you're absolutely certain you're wanted there. It's a terrific way to make a terrible first impression.

MOST BODY LANGUAGE IS COMMON SENSE

I can't think of any one isolated aspect of body language that can be interpreted with accuracy. Most body language must be read in context with the total situation. For example, folded arms might indicate that an individual is defiant or defensive. It also might mean that he or she is tired, or bored or is chilly and trying to generate warmth. Some experts say that folded arms indicate a resistance to a message, while others say it could just as well indicate that a listener is paying close attention to the speaker's every word.

When interpreting body language, the total person must be "read" for accurate assumptions. A person who stands with hands on hips could be interpreted as being cocky or arrogant. This might be a correct assumption. On the other hand, the individual might suffer from a backache and be using his or her hands as support.

But when reading a person in total context, posture generally will reveal a great deal about self-image and self-esteem. People who hold their heads erect and their bodies straight generally are self-assured. Again, the total picture must be viewed. Is the person merely putting up a front to compensate for a low self-image? By comparing the posture with personality, we can often determine what we need to know.

By the same token, people whose eyes are downcast and whose postures leave much to be desired might suffer from poor self-images.

Then again, they might have just received information that has troubled them greatly. Again, reading the total situation can help us assess the individual.

BODY LANGUAGE FOR FIRST IMPRESSIONS

There is probably not a single point in any relationship where body language is more significant than on a first meeting. Once two people get to know each other, they don't feel a need to attach a high degree of significance to posture. Remember, minds are made up about people within four to 10 seconds.

So it's important that your body gives off the right signals at a first meeting. We've already discussed the importance of giving a firm handshake, but that's just the first step. Let's examine other important points to keep in mind about body language when meeting another.

(1) **Pay attention.** This means actively listening to what he or she has to say and letting your body reveal your attention by sitting or standing erect. Eye contact is essential.

(2) **Add power to your points.** Even though your words might make a point, they very well could be lost on your listener unless your body indicates the point's significance. Good posture and strong (but not overly dramatic) gestures will help add power to your statements.

(3) **Remain calm.** While sitting, some people can't seem to resist shuffling their feet, crossing their legs or drumming their fingers. Of course, all these actions indicate disinterest, while the person might, in fact, be extremely nervous. Be aware of your hands and feet, and keep

them still when not in use. And, by all means, avoid any nervous habits or gestures, such as fingernail-biting or hair twisting.

(4) **Relax your face.** The face is usually a giveaway to a person's true thoughts. The eyebrows alone can indicate anger, surprise, fear, doubts, skepticism, disbelief and confusion. Coupled with smiles and frowns, a face can be an open book.

Be aware that your body often speaks as loudly as your words. To make your points satisfactorily, it's vital for your body to reinforce your words. It's not only critical for making first impressions, but it's a fine communication skill that can increase your effectiveness throughout life.

So let's move on to the next chapter on manners—the icing on the cake for making first impressions. No matter how well you look and how competent you are, your behavior still will be critiqued by new people. Manners are skills that can help us keep on our best behavior.

CHAPTER HIGHLIGHTS

(1) Experts say 70% to 80% of all communication is nonverbal. Our words might convey our thoughts, but people look at our faces and bodies for the real story.

(2) Common non-verbal communication skills include eye contact, nodding approval, smiling, touching and hand-shakes.

(3) Personal space is the two feet extending around a person. Except in crowded conditions, it should not be violated.

(4) Most body language is common sense and must be read in context with the total personality.

(5) Body language skills for first encounters include paying attention through active listening and attentive posture, letting your posture reflect the significance of your points, remaining calm and relaxing your face.

MY PERSONAL ACTION PLAN

** The most important idea I gained from reading this chapter is: _____

_____ .

** My plan for using this idea is: _____

_____ .

** I will commit to this idea because: _____

_____ .

** The specific actions I will take to implement this idea are: _____

_____

_____ .

** The results I expect from my usage of this idea are: ___

_____

_____ .

Chapter Eleven

Mind Your Manners

We scarcely note and quickly forget the crude street bum, because a bum is supposed to behave like a bum. But when someone in a business setting acts like a boor, we seldom forget.

That's why practicing good manners is extremely critical to making a favorable first impression. What good is it to wear a $500 suit to a dinner, if you behave like a cave dweller?

We often talk about manners and etiquette as if they are archaic rituals we only practice for tradition's sake. Sometimes, we even view them as a form of self-punishment, because we feel they inhibit us from being our true selves. But nothing could be farther from the truth.

Can you imagine living in a culture where individuals did exactly what suited them, regardless of the tastes and desires of others?

MANNERS ARE A FORM OF COMMUNICATION

When people practice good manners, they are communicating respect for the people they're with. They're expressing the hope that their interactions will be smooth. So, in a way, a display of good manners amounts to a high compliment.

A display of poor manners, however, sends the opposite message. Let me share with you a personal experience. The owner of a business once invited me to speak at a company banquet, and I accepted the invitation. At the event, I was seated at the table with the owner and some of his friends. While I didn't consider myself a "guest of honor" who required exceptional treatment, I certainly felt that my presence as an outsider might have prompted good behavior from the group.

I was wrong. And, quite frankly, I was appalled at the circumstances that unfolded in my presence. As someone who was unfamiliar with the group, I wanted to feel that I was welcomed and would have preferred to have felt comfortable seated at the table with the company VIP's. But instead of acting pleased with what I had to say, one of the owner's staff was continually argumentative. Talk about building a rapport!

But it was the behavior of my host—the company owner—which made the biggest impression. I've never seen a more prominent display of boorish behavior in my life. He was an extremely successful man in terms of his career and finances. Yet, he ate as if he belonged in a zoo. He held his gravy-covered roast beef with his fingers, and he tore into his food with such gusto that, at one point, I actually thought he was going to put his foot on the table to hold down the meat he was ripping apart with his hands. He was constantly licking his fingers. And, occasionally, I'd see him reach over to his wife's plate to eat her food, too.

I was amazed! Here was a good example of a man who looked like he belonged with the jet set, but he acted like he belonged on skid row. He might have looked impressive, but his choice of manners showed him for a boor.

True, the man was a financial success; he had gotten to where he wanted to be in the business world. And odds are very good he will continue to be successful, will continue to earn a high level of income and will enjoy a certain degree of respect from his peers. But he short-changed himself through his choice of manners, because what do you think most people think of the man? For a brief answer, very little. Also, what kind of role model do you think he was to his subordinates?

And finally, didn't the man give me great gossip material to spread around the area, if I were inclined to gossip? Who is so successful that he or she can afford that type of publicity?

So, in the final analysis, a display of good manners is more than just showing respect for others. It's showing respect for yourself—that you guard your reputation so closely that you'll not give others ammunition to use against you. And, in that regard, it's just plain good business.

Studies show that most people choose to do business with a particular firm because they like the people involved with it. If that's true—and my personal experience indicates that it is—then practicing good manners is a way of showing people that we like and respect them. And by treating them that way, we can hopefully get people to like and respect us in return.

COMMON SENSE MANNERS

Manners aren't mere traditions without foundations. Like body language and selection of clothes, it is really a matter of common sense. Let's examine proper etiquette for various situations to see if you don't agree.

(1) **Introductions.** This is frequently an uncomfortable circumstance for many individuals. Whom do you introduce first? Always direct your first introduction to the most important or elder of two persons. For example, if you must introduce your boss to a friend, speak first to the boss. "Mr. Jones, I'd like you to meet my friend, Julia Richards." To speak first to the person of lesser importance would be making the more important person wait for information. When you must introduce people of perceived equal status, always present the person accompanying you to the person you encounter. This suggests an air of importance to the person not in your company.

(2) **Referring to superiors.** If you've been invited to call your superiors by their first names, go ahead. Otherwise, it's "Mr. Smith" or Ms. Jones," unless a woman would prefer "Mrs." or "Miss." Even if they call you by your first name, do not assume you have the same liberty. Again, it's simply a matter of deferring to age, maturity and experience.

(3) **Introducing yourself.** Unless you are absolutely certain that a person knows your first and last name, don't wait for him or her to introduce you. It could prove to be an embarrassing experience for both of you if the person can't readily recall your name. Besides, introducing yourself by simply stating your name and profession gives you an air of importance. It's a subtle, tasteful way of proclaiming you're proud of who you are.

(4) **Thank-you notes.** These should be sent promptly upon receiving a gift, a favor of significance or after having attended a social function. To fail to acknowledge formally an expression of kindness is a blatant faux pas.

132

(5) **Smoking.** If there are not ashtrays present, it might be a good idea to assume that smoking isn't permitted. You can always ask permission, if you feel comfortable with your host. But if anyone present should ask if you would refrain, by all manes, do so. Some people have a distaste for cigarette smoke, and others are allergic to it.

(6) **Jokes.** They're fine if they are tasteful and appropriate to the situation. Otherwise, forget them—especially if there is even the slightest doubt that a particular gag might be offensive to someone present.

(7) **Conversation.** Being a pleasant conversationalist calls for several guidelines. First, do not be a monomaniac. The person who can talk only about one topic will quickly be rated as boring. Second, don't monpolize a conversation. Always allow others to air views. Third, encourage others to talk by asking them questions pertaining to their fields, families or interests. Not only does this ensure that all people contribute to a conversation, but asking a person to talk on a topic that he or she finds interesting is a high compliment. And finally, never ask prying questions. It can prove to be an embarrassing situation for both of you.

(8) **Invitations.** Always reply promptly to these. If someone thinks enough of you to request your presence, you should honor them with a prompt reply, regardless of whether you can actually attend. And don't assume that getting an invitation automatically entitles you to bring a guest.

(9) **Compliments.** When you get one, respond with a simple—but genuine—"thank you." Too often, people feel as if they must devalue themselves when someone pays them a compliment. First, it's unnecessary.

Second, devaluing yourself indirectly suggests to the person who complimented you that his or her taste is in question. And third, why should a person advertise insecurity? A simple "thank you" is quite sufficient for a compliment. If you feel the need to say anything else, you might say how nice it is for the person to have offered the compliment. You might even return the compliment with one of your own—provided that the compliment you return is sincere. Otherwise, forget it. The person will know he or she is being patronized.

(10) **Show of affection among co-workers.** Handshakes are fine. So is a touch on the arm or shoulder. But kissing is seldom if ever appropriate. There is too much of a possibility that it might be misconstrued. In business, the appearance of impropriety can be as destructive and devastating as the real thing.

(11) **Table manners.** I'm sure you've heard these before. We usually get our first lesson in proper etiquette at the dinner table as children. But, just in case the business owner I mentioned previously in this chapter happens to be reading this, I'll restate the obvious. Know the proper usage of all utensils and do so properly. If you are unsure, resist calling attention to yourself and gently observe the actions of others in the group whom you trust. Resist the temptation to talk with food in your mouth. If you must talk while chewing, at least have the decency to hold a napkin in front of your mouth so you won't offend others who must look at you. Bread should be broken into a bite-sized piece, buttered if preferred then eaten. This is a more delicate action than chomping into a piece of bread and getting butter all over your mouth. And wipe your mouth before drinking, lest you leave traces of your dinner on the rim of your beverage glass for the entire

party to behold. And, by all means, don't wolf your food. Not only will you make a spectacle of yourself, but it's extremely difficult to make pleasant dinner conversation while trying to set a personal speed record for consumption of a meal.

Doesn't it all seem like common sense? I believe it is. Of course, I've only touched the tip of the iceberg when it comes to protocol. But for a general guideline, I have to point to the golden rule—do unto others as you'd have others do unto you. And when dealing with people from different cultures, I'd recommend the platinum rule—do unto others as they would have you do unto them. You might have to research their customs to know how to interact effectively with them, but I promise you, your time will be well spent.

And to close this section on making first impressions, I might advise you to remember that good etiquette often is nothing more than assisting a person in need. When you see a situation where you can be of service to someone, it will rarely if ever hurt you to lend a hand. Most of the time, you'll make a fantastic impression that won't be easily forgotten. But do so gently so as to not embarrass the person you are assisting.

So now we'll move on to the next section dealing with professional competence. And the first chapter in that section represents a natural progression from etiquette. The subject is getting along with people— an important requirement for anyone who must work with or for others.

CHAPTER HIGHLIGHTS

(1) Practicing good etiquette is a way of showing interest in another person. Good manners are a sign of respect for

the person you are with and the occasion that you're a part of.

(2) When people choose to practice good manners, they are communicating that they respect the people they're with and feel they are important enough to be on their best behavior so that interpersonal interaction will be smooth.

(3) A display of good manners shows self-respect in that you guard your reputation so closely that you'll not give others ammunition to use against you. It's also good business, because people don't win clients by alienating them.

(4) Manners aren't mere traditions without foundations. Like body language and selection of clothes, it is really a matter of common sense.

(5) Good etiquette is basically remembering the golden and platinum rules and assisting a person in need.

MY PERSONAL ACTION PLAN

** The most important idea I gained from reading this chapter is: _____

_____ .

** My plan for using this idea is: _____

_____ .

** I will commit to this idea because: _____

_____ .

** The specific actions I will take to implement this idea are: _____

_____

_____.

** The results I expect from my usage of this idea are: ____

_____

_____.

Section III

PROFESSIONAL COMPETENCE

Chapter Twelve

People Skills

It's nice to look nice. It's even nicer to behave nicely. And it's absolutely wonderful to have a strong self-image. But, in the final analysis, whether you sink or swim in the professional world depends primarily on two things—how good you are at what you do and how well you get along with others.

It goes without saying that you've got to be able to perform well in your profession. So let's focus on the other career requirement—interacting effectively with others, which, in some respects, is even more important. Unfortunately, the world is filled with extremely competent people who did not advance to their potential solely because they wouldn't or did not know how to treat people with dignity and respect.

In addition to being good at what we are, it's vital to be good at who we are. We must have the skills, abilities and attitudes necessary for total effectiveness. People who allow the development of career skills to overshadow their interactive development run a big chance of stunting their own growth—if not of actually committing career suicide.

No matter what you do, you have to work with others. Whether they include customers, co-workers or superiors—or all three—the same rules apply. People don't want to do business or work with people who offend them. And the world offers too many other career/ business options for anyone to stand for shabby treatment.

In other words, all the talents, skills and abilities in the world relating to your chosen field won't be enough for real success without sufficient people skills. We must be "enough" as people before we can possibly interact effectively with others. So until we are enough, nothing else will ever be enough.

WHO'S OK?

Why do people treat others the way they do? A popular theory behind human interaction offers a fine explanation. Let's examine the four basic types of interaction between two people.

(1) **I'm OK, You're OK.** This is the essence of all positive interaction. People with strong self-images automatically treat others well, because they feel good about themselves. They're accustomed to treating others with dignity and respect, because they have high self-esteem, which means they treat themselves the same way. When such treatment is returned, the foundation for a positive, healthy relationship is formed.

(2) **I'm OK, You're Junk.** People who operate from this mindset usually make more enemies than friends. If you remember the comedy team of Abbott and Costello, who were in their heyday during the 1940's, you'll probably recall that this often was the basis for slick Bud Abbott's treatment of his short, fat, simple-minded

stooge. Despite the fact that the two supposedly were "pals," Abbott was forever slapping Costello and setting him up for the "short-end of the stick" in any situation. In reality, this philosophy appeals to people who don't have a healthy self-image. Because they don't feel good about themselves, they choose to compensate by treating others shabbily. It's the old "I-can-raise-myself-by-kicking-you-down" outlook on life that's common among spouse and child abusers—whether the abuse is physically or emotionally.

(3) **I'm Junk, You're OK.** On the other side of the coin, this is the mindset of spouses who stand for abusive treatment. Children who are abused might come to adopt this philosophy over time. In the comedy world, Lou Costello was the perfect foil for Bud Abbott because this was his frame of reference. He would stand for the abuse because he felt he deserved it. The Lou Costellos of the world, who also have poor self-images, are worse off than the Bud Abbotts, who at least try to cover their weaknesses through a facade of strength. The Costellos of the world merely admit they are junk and rarely make any effort to break out of that mindset.

(4) **We're both junk.** You've heard it said that there is no honor among thieves. This is true because thieves generally function with a we're-both-junk mindset. One of the best ways to ruin a self-image is through dishonesty. People who make dishonesty a daily practice generally don't think much of themselves, and they don't think much of others like them.

Obviously, there is only one acceptable mindset for success—holding yourself and others in high esteem. Any other outlook won't promote harmony and effective interaction.

YOU CAN'T CONTROL

Of course, we can only control the way we treat others. We can't control the way they treat us. Certainly, we don't have to put up with shabby treatment from "friends" (the kind who eliminate your need for enemies). But when it comes to the work setting, we might not be able to separate ourselves from irritating, antagonistic peers, short of firing them, if we have the authority.

But firing, of course, is—or should be—a last-resort method. First, firing is expensive. All the resources invested in the individual's development is lost. And second, it's a shame to lose someone if he or she does good work. Instead of firing, it's more productive—and easier on the nerves—to improve their behavior.

But didn't I just say that you can't control another's behavior? That's true. But you can certainly create an atmosphere conducive to change. To better understand how this is done, let's first look at the various barriers that prevent people from changing their behavior.

(1) **Not knowing how to seek alternatives.** People who are rigid in their thinking might not be as dogmatic as they are uninformed. Perhaps they're not aware that a better alternative exists, they don't know how to look for other alternatives. Of course, I realize that this isn't the excuse for all narrow-minded people, but it might well apply to some that you know.

(2) **Not knowing how to get cooperation from others.** People who are brusque and bossy also might be operating from the standpoint of ignorance. They don't know any other way to relate to people. If you know people like this, perhaps you can serve as an effective role model for changing their behavior.

(3) **Not knowing what we really want to do.** When people are engaged in the wrong profession, internal resentment can build. This resentment often is manifested in behavior.

(4) **Belief that we don't deserve better.** This is the Lou Costello syndrome. People who have poor self-images think so little of themselves that they truly believe they deserve the shabby treatment they get from others. It never dawns on them to make new friends or, in the case of battered spouses, to seek new companions because they believe they'd get the same treatment from anyone.

(5) **Fear of rejection.** Some people are afraid to be open in their interpersonal dealings with others for fear of rejection. They feel that treating people with respect, only to be rejected, would wound them deeply. Again, it's a matter of poor self-image.

(6) **Fear of change.** The longer a behavioral pattern has been established, the harder it will be to break. Many chain smokers and problem drinkers don't even try to break their habits because they fear life without their accustomed "crutch." Likewise, a person who is accustomed to being abusive, uncooperative or belligerent might find it difficult to interact sensitively with others.

(7) **Need to defend current behavior.** The longer a behavioral pattern has been established, the greater the need to defend it. People with weak self-images often look at abandoning a behavior as an admission of "guilt." Rather than change, they'll find ways to justify their behaviors, and simply maintaining them is one way to do that.

Change is a difficult thing for people to engineer in themselves. Yet, it's something that entrepreneurs of all types must deal with to live a full life. Everything is subject to change, and the effective person must be able to cope with changes.

Likewise, entrepreneurs will be more effective if they can help others effect change, or create an atmosphere conducive to change. This is done by helping others improve, or change, their self-image. Let's examine the process.

(A) **You are an influence.** It's important to realize that you are an influence on the person whose self-image you're trying to build. How much of an influence you are depends on how big a role you play in the person's life. Also, to believe that you aren't an influence is negative thinking. If you consider that you aren't an influence, you won't try to help the person change.

(B) **Change takes place slowly.** Although you're an influence, remember that you're only one influence. There are many more factors that affect a person's life. Be patient, and keep working toward your goal. Although the legendary tortoise was slow, he won the race by making small strides at a steady rate.

(C) **Acknowledge positive efforts.** If you don't, you can be certain there will be few, if any, repeat performances. Gaining approval from peers and superiors is a prime motivator for most people. If approval is withheld, so is the incentive to improve.

Unfortunately, in our society, people often get more attention for their mistakes than for their successes. When this happens, a person's self-confidence can be lowered through personal devaluing. It's important for us to recognize strengths to build others' self-confidence. Identify people's positive attributes and support them. When this is done, your compliments can't be interpreted as mere flattery or patronization, and the listener is sincerely complimented. As a result, his or her confidence and self-esteem will soar. This will have a positive impact on the person's self-image, which can lead to even greater performance.

(D) **Be aware of others' individual needs.** Believe it or not, there are some things people need more than money. Recognition for good performance, the freedom to participate in decisions affecting them and getting sensitive guidance will motivate some people more than cash. All three can have a positive impact on a person's self-image.

(E) **Talk to others with respect.** Remember that people have identities beyond their jobs. They have families, outside interests and dreams that often have nothing to do with the company. By learning more about the total person, you can discover ways to boost his or her self-image.

(F) **Be a good listener.** It's important that we understand what people tell us. Sometimes, it's even more important to listen "beyond the words" to what a person might want to say, but can't—or won't. Several years ago when I was teaching high school, there was a student named Donna whom I came to know very well. She was a favorite among teachers—at least she certainly was with me. A very positive young lady, she was active in sports, student government and a host of other extracurricular activities. She was a "mother hen" to her closest friends, and almost an automatic friend to everyone else. Just being in her presence would lift dampened spirits. If she had enemies, I didn't know them, and I was in a position to know just about everything pertaining to my students. At least I thought

I was until I received a telephone call one morning that Donna had committed suicide.

I did not understand it then, and I still do not. Her whole life had been in front of her. Yet, she chose to end it. Donna was one of the most positive people I had ever met. It was hard to believe someone of her maturity was an adolescent. We had become very close—yet, I never knew there was a problem. As far as I could tell, there was no cause for sorrow in her history. Obviously, I was wrong. And while I don't blame myself for her death, I feel that if I had listened beyond her words, perhaps I could have "heard" that she was hurting and that something was terribly wrong in her life. Then, maybe I could have helped her make a different decision.

Persons with good people skills take listening seriously. I promise you, I do. It's the lesson I learned from Donna.

(F) **Make the building of others' self-image a regular part of your job.** By making this commitment, not only can you strengthen people's self-images and, thus, increase their effectiveness, but you'll be amazed at the fringe benefits that come with it. You'll be better valued, better respected and better admired.

In other words, by building others' self-images, you build your own in the process. That's not a bad return on your investment, is it?

I'm sure you've heard of the "golden rule"—do unto others as you'd have others do unto you. I'd like to recommend the "platinum rule"—do unto others as others would have you do unto them. Find out how people like to be treated, and treat them that way. The results can be truly significant when you react to people on their own terms.

COMMUNICATION IS ESSENTIAL FOR GOOD TREATMENT

I talked earlier about effective listening, and how a person should listen beyond a message to determine its significance. I stand by that advice. But, at the same time, I would advise you to avoid misunderstandings by making your messages so clear that your words will speak for themselves.

Effective communication is power. It's making your point in a manner that's easily understood. Ineffective communication leads to misunderstandings, mistakes, confusion and, sometimes, trouble. Most conflicts result from ineffective communication. One person misunderstands another, and ill will develops.

When people don't make themselves clear to their listeners, there is usually a cause. Let's examine some routine causes of ineffective message delivery.

(1) **Providing incomplete information.** The omission of even the slightest bit of pertinent information can lead to trouble. If someone gives you a recipe but fails to include one ingredient, the end result might not be exactly what either of you had in mind.

(2) **Making assumptions.** When a person assumes that another knows certain information, he or she runs the risk of engineering a communications breakdown. Suppose I asked you to type a report and assumed you knew that I wanted it triple-spaced instead of the standard double-spacing used for most documents. Chances are good I wouldn't get what I wanted.

(3) **Using words with multiple meanings.** It has been said that the English language's 500 most common words have a total of 14,000 meanings. That's an average of

28 meanings per word! Take the word "plate." Its definitions include a dish, an arrangement of a meal, home base in baseball, a denture, engraving metal and a thin sheet of metal such as gold or silver. The word "trade" can mean an occupation of skilled work, all the persons in a particular business, commerce, customers, a purchase or sale or an exchange. When words with multiple definitions are used, there is the chance for miscommunication.

(4) **Poor choice of words.** Speakers might know what they intend to say. But unless they choose the correct words, they might actually say something else. Be careful to choose the words that appropriately convey your thought.

(5) **Unclear transitions.** When a speaker shifts a conversation from one topic to another, a listener can be misled if the transition isn't made clear. Let your listeners know when you're changing topics.

When communications go awry, the results can often be worse than if there had been no communication at all. Take pains to send clear messages. When working with others, your effectiveness depends on it.

GETTING FEEDBACK

As a listener, how can you be sure that others' messages accurately convey their thoughts? You can't be sure, unless you check your understanding of the message with the speaker. This is the process of getting feedback.

Checking your understanding of a message with the speaker can avoid communication breakdowns. If your understanding is correct, the communication process is complete. If it isn't, then you've informed the speaker that the process wasn't satisfactorily completed. As a result, the speaker gets another chance to send his or her message.

Get into the habit of feeding back messages to speakers. And when you're the speaker, don't be afraid to ask for feedback to ensure that your message was understood the way you intended it to be. This simple process can avoid a lot of trouble that otherwise might result from miscommunication.

For anyone sincerely interested in improving his or her communication skills, the quality of their relationships and self-promotional skills, I highly recommend the Dale Carnegie Course.

I had the great pleasure of participating in Dale Carnegie Training and can tell you first-hand that the Sponsors, Instructors and Graduate Assistants are deeply interested in you as a person and in the development of you in your personal and professional lives. Under their direction and effective role-modeling, I observed the tremendous growth of people skills and leadership skills in myself and fellow class members.

Any success I have had in these areas I credit to the people involved in the Dale Carnegie Course. I should mention that the training also offers a myriad of other wonderful benefits.

This chapter has dealt primarily with people skills that can benefit anyone in any position, from the front-line employee who has an eye on a higher post, all the way up to the chief executive of an organization.

The next chapter offers advice and suggestions for leaders or would-be leaders.

CHAPTER HIGHLIGHTS

(1) Successful interaction is based on holding yourself and others in high esteem.

151

(2) Although you can't control the way others behave, you can create an atmosphere conducive to behavior change.

(3) Various reasons why people resist changing their behavior include not knowing how to seek alternatives, not knowing how to get others' cooperation, not knowing what we really want to do, belief we don't deserve better, fear of rejection, fear of change and a need to defend current behavior.

(4) Help others change behavior by realizing that you are an influence and that change occurs slowly. Acknowledge positive efforts, be aware of individuals' needs, talk to them as people, be a good listener. And make the building of self-image a regular part of your job.

(5) Communication is an essential part of relating to people. Some reasons why people often don't make themselves clear include providing incomplete information, making assumptions, using words with multiple meanings, poor choice of words and making unclear transitions.

(6) Feedback, or the process of repeating what you understand, is an excellent way to prevent communication breakdowns.

MY PERSONAL ACTION PLAN

** The most important idea I gained from reading this chapter is: _____

_____.

** My plan for using this idea is: _____

_____.

** I will commit to this idea because: _____

_____ .

** The specific actions I will take to implement this idea
are: _____

_____

_____ .

** The results I expect from my usage of this idea are: ___

_____

_____ .

Chapter Thirteen

Learning to Lead

Leadership abilities are like people skills in that they involve smooth interaction with people. But what separates leadership skills from people skills is that leadership skills are designed to influence others to take the course of action you choose.

In that respect, leadership abilities are certainly assets for managers. But this doesn't mean there's nothing of benefit for the person who isn't a leader by position. As I stated in the previous chapter, the best way to become qualified for a leadership position is to learn how a leader acts.

But more importantly, this chapter will benefit you, no matter what career role you play, because virtually everyone acts as a leader at some time or another. If you're a parent, you're a leader. If you head a volunteer organization, you're a leader. Likewise if you're appointed to chair any kind of committee or panel, be it in a business, church or civic arena, you'll be acting as a leader.

Since the odds are pretty good that you will serve as a leader at some point in your life, it is a good idea to learn how its done— if only to be prepared when the time comes.

WHAT IS LEADERSHIP

Dwight David Eisenhower, the 34th president of the United States, once said, "Leadership is the art of getting someone else to do something that you want done because he wants to do it." Eisenhower, of course, was no stranger to leadership. In addition to being the nation's chief executive, he also served as a general in the military during World War II. Eisenhower often demonstrated the art of leadership by placing a rope on a table and pointing out that a person could push it all day, but the rope would go nowhere. On the other hand, if a person were to pull the rope, it would follow with ease. The same principle applies with people.

If you push people, they might push back. There's no progress in that scenario. But if you lead them, you can go wherever you like.

Leadership is getting people to do what they don't want to do or don't think they are capable of doing, and therefore, might not be motivated to do. Perhaps, leading people might be a way of convincing them of their own strengths and abilities, or transforming them from exhibiting a negative attitude to having a positive attitude and, as a result, getting them to willingly engage in projects they might otherwise dread or reject.

Using the word "leader" as an acronym, let's examine what makes a good leader.

(L) **A leader is a listener.** We mentioned this in the previous chapter, but this trait can't be stressed too much.

156

Listening carefully to the spoken and "hidden" word is essential in leadership positions. Leaders must have a keen ability to read people. This helps in negotiations of all types. Listening also helps leaders gauge the effectiveness of individual subordinates on any given day, since we're all prone to have our ups and downs.

(E) **A leader is enthusiastic.** Given the choice between two subordinates, whom would you choose—one who is enthusiastic about the job or one who isn't? I think the choice is clear, and it goes double for leaders. Enthusiasm is having the ability to determine ambitions and then maintaining the attitude required to pursue them. It's difficult to impossible to lead any effort that doesn't excite you. Effective leaders can find something exciting about any effort—no matter how large or small—that pertains to the cause. If a job is integral to the big picture, it's worth getting excited about. Also, enthusiasm is contagious. A leader excited about a cause will stand a better chance of exciting subordinates than one who has a hard time staying awake.

(A) **A leader is an advertiser.** The eyes of subordinates are always upon their leader. Effective leaders serve as role models by the way they present themselves, both in terms of image and effectiveness, and in the way they behave. When a leader provides a good example, he or she can inspire followers. If the leader offers a poor example, the cause very well might be lost.

(D) **A leader is decisive.** Indecisiveness sends a signal to subordinates that their leader is weak. Indecisive leaders

157

also breed indecisive subordinates. Leaders cannot dawdle and delay when its time for a decision. Good ones form the habit of reviewing all available information, then making a decision they can live with. Effective leaders are slow to change their minds once they've decided an issue.

(E) **A leader engages with others.** Leaders like to get to know their subordinates on a personal as well as a professional level. They don't necessarily desire to be "buddies," but they do not hesitate to relate to their subordinates on personal levels. After all, leaders who truly care for their subordinates will have subordinates who truly care for them—and will work harder for them, too.

(R) **A leader is a reinforcer of strengths.** Leaders encourage continued development by recognizing and complimenting subordinates for their strengths. It's important to recognize subordinates' strengths, because people often don't recognize strengths in themselves. By calling their strengths to people's attention, we can boost their confidence and self-image. Both parties prosper through positive reinforcement, which often creates a win-win situation. The subordinate wins by developing increased effectiveness and a greater sense of self-worth, and the leader wins by generating increased results through the building of stronger subordinates. The leader's encouraging remarks enable the subordinate to work to do an even better job, and the resulting boost in self-confidence will flood over into other areas where more development is needed.

A leader is no better than his or her followers. By building them effectively, leaders also build themselves.

A LEADER'S AREA OF EFFECTIVENESS

There are three basic areas where leaders must be effective: personal characteristics, the ability to break down superficial barriers and the ability to create an environment conducive to growth. Let's examine each area.

PERSONAL CHARACTERISTICS

The same traits that make anyone effective also apply to leaders, people who serve in greater capacities. They must have a positive self-image and be capable in their area. They are motivated by values—to focus on means more than ends.

But leaders also must be able to inspire others to motivate themselves. They must have the ability to help others see what they can be and then be able to "light a fire" under them to help them realize their ambitions.

Leaders are also coaches. They have the ability to demonstrate skills to subordinates and help them develop these skills to maximum proficiency.

Also important is the fact that leaders be nonjudgmental and not carry preconceived concepts of other individuals. A good leader starts with a clean slate with each person and forms impressions based on the way subordinates behave—not the way the leader thinks individuals might behave. This is vital to ensure high productivity.

When people in leadership positions "size up" their subordinates before getting to know them, they run the risk of attaching "labels" to them that will be hard to shake. When a person in authority labels someone—either in positive or negative terms—the subordinate who respects the leader—if only by position—tends to accept such typing as truth.

The law of self-fulfilling prophecy can be a powerful tool when applied positively. Unfortunately, it works just as well negatively, and it can be a destructive force in that direction. Effective leaders are careful not to attach negative labels to subordinates.

And, finally, leaders have a professional image. It all goes back to appearance. Image doesn't "make" people, but it can certainly break them. Leaders cannot earn respect from subordinates if the superiors' images aren't in keeping with their abilities and positions.

THE ABILITY TO BREAK DOWN SUPERFICIAL BARRIERS

People skills allow leaders to interact effectively with others. They don't have the time or energy to employ defense mechanisms that can only hamper positive interaction. They practice the golden rule only when they don't know enough about an individual to practice its platinum counterpart—to treat others the way they would have you treat them.

They learn about people's outside lives, including their families and interests. By showing a sincere interest in a person's non-work life, leaders develop empathy and can better relate to their subordinates.

Finally, effective leaders communicate by touching, but only when communicating positively. They don't use physical contact for criticism or reproach. But a pat on the shoulder or on the back can go a long way to augment words of praise.

Touching is a powerful means of communication. Psychologists report that people who are not touched at an early age don't develop as well as those who enjoyed close, warm physical contact. And touching's benefits still apply even when we become adults. Although it's sometimes frowned upon in our society, touching—within proper limits, of course—is a very sincere form of communication.

CREATING AN ENVIRONMENT CONDUCIVE TO GROWTH

Leaders create environments conducive to prosperity for all members. Let's take a look at the components of such an environment.

(1) **It must be positive.** A positive atmosphere is the foundation for productivity. People must be able to have fun while they work if they are to enjoy working. An occasional party or celebration following significant achievements can pay off in rich dividends in morale, incentive and job satisfaction.

(2) **It must be comfortable.** The best work is done in comfort, which means that physical comforts must be provided. Comfortable chairs in well-lighted and well-equipped work stations is essential. Temperature control is also a major factor. It's difficult to be productive when you're freezing—or roasting.

(3) **Ambitions must be defined and shared.** Before subordinates can achieve ambitions, they first must know what they are. Second, they must know how they'll benefit for achieving them. When leaders and subordinates genuinely share ambitions, the unit itself becomes a powerful force that stands a good chance of being successful. Ambitions must be realistic to be achieved, but they also must be high to be challenging. When ambitions aren't challenging, subordinates can become frustrated and demotivated.

(4) **Leaders enable subordinates to know their jobs.** Obviously, an ambition can't be realized if a person doesn't know how to do what it takes to achieve it. Effective leaders are ready, willing and able to help their followers

become as proficient as possible at their jobs. They don't belittle subordinates for not knowing proper procedure; instead, they teach it—over and over again, if necessary. The process involves a great deal of coaching. The leader explains the job, demonstrates how it is done, allows the subordinate to perform, then offers advice for improvement.

(5) **Leaders allow interaction.** Leaders allow subordinates to offer input into matters that affect them and their job performance. Keeping subordinates satisfied is a key to getting the job done. This is not to say that leaders grant subordinates' every request, but they do stand willing to listen to any ideas subordinates might have. It's a practice that leads to growth for all parties involved.

By creating an environment conducive to growth, leaders exert a positive influence over their subordinates that helps them succeed— both for the organization and themselves.

CRITICISM

Although leaders try to avoid criticism, there are times when it's absolutely unavoidable. But when applied in a confirming fashion, criticism can be a positive, growth experience for the subordinate.

When criticizing, it's a good idea to offer a compliment, if at all appropriate. Again, it must be a sincere compliment. Flattery is transparent as glass. If two sincere compliments can be delivered, then I would suggest sandwiching the criticism between the compliments. The first compliment will place the individual in a positive frame of mind to receive the criticism, and the second compliment will leave the individual with something positive. Together, the two compliments will put the individual in a better frame of mind for improving, and they'll also show the individual that the leader sincerely values his or her overall contributions.

When considering offering criticism to a subordinate, ask yourself six questions. I strongly suggest that the person in question be asked to join you in a conversation. Explain that something obviously is amiss and that "**together** we can perhaps come to a resolution."

(1) **Is the individual in a position to receive the criticism positively?** If the person has had a terrible week or is battling with a host of other demands, it might be a good idea to postpone the critique until a time when the individual might be able to receive it better.

(2) **Am I willing to hear the fallout?** When criticism is delivered, the critiqued individual often will feel the need to defend himself or herself. Sometimes, it will take a lot of time and effort to deal with the fallout. If you're not ready to deal with it, perhaps now is not the time to criticize.

(3) **Is it the first time the individual will hear the critique?** If so, offering the critique might not be painful. I've found that many people don't mind criticism, because it's an opportunity for them to improve. However, if this is the 17th time the criticism is to be delivered, perhaps giving it might consume more breath than is warranted. A better decision might be whether to live with the problem or dismiss the problem-causer.

(4) **Can the individual improve?** Obviously, there is no profit to critiquing an individual who is not in a position to improve. Before criticizing, be certain that the individual isn't working beyond his or her abilities.

(5) **Am I causing the problem?** Recall your previous communications with the individual. Could you have miscommunicated orders? Is there a personality clash between the two of you?

(6) **Is the individual able to learn through other means?** Sometimes, criticism isn't necessary to bring a point home. An illustration or a story can be a fine metaphor to make a point without ruffling feathers.

Criticism is a fine tool to help subordinates grow, but it should be used sparingly. Too much can be counterproductive. Before issuing criticism, take pains to make sure it's presented in a tactful, appropriate manner and that, if at all possible, the subordinate is in a positive frame of mind to receive it.

LEADERS HAVE INTEGRITY

The achieving of an ambition is only of secondary importance to an effective leader, who is always most concerned with the means to the end. For example, starting a personal business might be important, but if start-up capital must be obtained through illegal means, the effective leader isn't interested.

Values are more than just honorable words to drop in the presence of others. They are codes of life to which effective leaders fully subscribe. They're sort of like rules to a game that must be followed if the game is to be rewarding and any fun at all.

People who must get ahead at all costs have lost control of their lives. Their ambition is in charge, and it dictates to them what they will do to achieve it. But people who have values are in charge of their own lives. Their ambitions are important, but they decide what they will and won't do to pursue it. For example, becoming a CEO of a major corporation might be your burning ambition, but I doubt very much that you would accelerate your pursuit by murdering the current person in charge.

Values are important to all of us. But if you are a leader, your values will be assessed and very likely adopted by those who would follow you. So it's vital for your values to reflect the values you would have them adopt.

LEADERS HAVE DISCIPLINE

Leaders must have the discipline to achieve their ambitions within the framework of their values and their plans. There's no one standing over their shoulder to make sure it gets done. If they don't take responsibility for their success, they won't succeed.

Taking responsibility is simply a matter of developing the discipline or self-control. I like Bobby Knight's definition of discipline—"Doing what has to be done. Doing it when it has to be done. Doing it as well as it can be done. Doing it that way all the time."

Ambitions require the fuel of work and accomplishment to keep them alive. A person is charged by his or her own success along the way and is encouraged to work even harder. Ambition without discipline is nothing more than fantasy. Without the drive to do what is necessary to achieve it, an ambition eventually will burn itself out.

Again, don't underestimate the significance of role modeling. A leader without discipline also may have followers without discipline, which will adversely affect the organization as a whole.

Worthwhile efforts demand discipline. Devote plenty to your ambitions for the best chance of success.

LEADERS ARE COMMITTED

Integrity and discipline are fine qualities for achieving ambitions, but commitment is the quality that counts. Without commitment, most ambitions would never be reached.

Commitment is a promise a person makes that an ambition will be achieved, unless he or she dies first. It's like saying that life without pursuit of the ambition isn't worth the living—or, at the very least, lacks the excitement that an entrepreneurial life should offer.

Life itself is for the enjoyment that comes with self-improvement and success. Commitments to those goals—whatever form they take— is what keeps us going.

But don't think that fulfilling a commitment is necessarily easy. Sometimes, it can be. And, other times, it can be terribly difficult. If you're willing to make a commitment and take a stand, then you'd better be willing to accept any hardships or personal sacrifices it might involve.

Commitment can be tough. But it can also be rewarding. Just remember that in history, literature and life itself, the protagonist is in continual opposition to the status quo and is continually in the process of becoming himself or herself. Through commitment to our ambitions, we become creative entrepreneurs who can eventually become heroes and heroines through achievement of ambitions.

As an advertisement for Shearson-Lehman/American Express read, "Commitment is the stuff character is made of—the power to change the face of things."

And another important quality for leadership is creativity. But rather than discussing that quality here, let's move on to the next chapter, where we can discuss it fully.

CHAPTER HIGHLIGHTS

(1) Good people skills deal primarily with typical, everyday interaction between people, while leadership skills focus primarily on relationships between superiors and subordinates.

(2) The best way to become qualified for a leadership position is to learn how a leader acts. Virtually everyone, at some time or another, acts as a leader.

(3) Leadership is the opposite of pushing. It's getting people to do what they don't want to do or don't think they are capable of doing, and therefore, might not be motivated to do. It's convincing people of their own strengths and abilities.

(4) Leaders are listeners, enthusiastic, advertisers, decisive, engage with others and reinforce strengths of others.

(5) A leader must be effective in personal characteristics, in the ability to break down superficial barriers and in creating an environment conducive to growth.

(6) When positive, criticism can be a good tool for growth.

(7) Leaders have integrity. They have discipline, and they are committed to getting results.

MY PERSONAL ACTION PLAN

** The most important idea I gained from reading this chapter is: _____

_____ .

** My plan for using this idea is: _____

_____ .

** I will commit to this idea because: _____

_____ .

** The specific actions I will take to implement this idea are: _____

_____

_____ .

** The results I expect from my usage of this idea are: ____

_____

_____ .

Chapter Fourteen

Developing Creativity

Do you know how McDonald's hamburger franchises began? A milkshake machine salesman named Ray Kroc came upon a popular California business owned and operated by the McDonald brothers. The business sold only 15-cent hamburgers, french fries, soft drinks and milkshakes and offered no dining facilities. Food was prepared for consumption in cars or off the premises, and demand for the food during lunch and dinner hours was phenomenal.

So Kroc bought franchising rights from the McDonalds and, slowly but surely, built the enterprise into a successful, booming nationwide business. But Kroc was an entrepreneur who wasn't satisfied just to leave well enough alone, because a long line of competitors kept cropping up to keep him on his toes. So he continued to lead his industry by expanding the McDonald's menu to include larger burgers, other types of sandwiches, several varieties of breakfast foods, salads, ice cream, cookies and pastries. As traffic increased below the golden arches, buildings expanded to allow indoor dining, and drive-through windows came into being for the convenience of the customer who didn't care to leave his or her car.

That was quite an evolution from its early days. But growth can cause problems, and the fast food industry was no exception to the rule. And the problem is the fact that fast food is no longer fast. I've waited longer in some fast-food lines than I have in some fine restaurants.

So what happens? Out in the Midwest, an entrepreneurial enterprise known as "Bargain Burgers" appears. The buildings are small— about the same size as fast-film-developing stands that aren't much bigger than broom closets. The menu is small; it includes burgers, fries and cold drinks. Food is prepared for off-site consumption, which means the business can keep its overhead to a minimum.

Does the idea sound familiar? Of course, it's nothing new. It's precisely the same idea that Ray Kroc used to build a multi-million dollar business. The brains behind Bargain Burgers simply recognized that the days of real fast food have been long gone. They dusted off McDonald's old idea to fill the void and bring back fast food.

Now, my question to you is, are the Bargain Burger people particularly creative? It depends on how you look at it. The idea certainly isn't new. But its application coupled with its timing has produced profitable results. Had the chain come into being during the late 1960's, it probably would have folded flat. At that time, America was enjoying the evolving hamburger chains of that day. But introduced during the 1980's, when fast food had degenerated to a memory, the idea caught on.

To me, that's creativity. Even if an idea is old, it sometimes can be used to produce a new result. After all, the idea wasn't original with Ray Kroc. Remember, he simply picked up the McDonald brothers' plan and made it work. But to say that Kroc wasn't creative because he didn't come up with the idea is like saying that Walt Disney wasn't creative because he didn't invent cartoons.

In business and in life, entrepreneurial creativity isn't so much coming up with new, original thoughts as it is putting old ideas to work, perhaps in a new way, and achieving successful results.

THE CREATIVITY "BLOCK"

For many years, I never thought of myself as a creative person. I didn't think I had the ability or knowledge to develop original ideas. And therein was my greatest barrier to developing creativity.

Remember, self-image is the key to all success and failure. And thinking that I wasn't creative was the best way to ensure that I never became creative. If key members of your environment tell you that you're dull and boring, chances are good you will become dull and boring. On the other hand, if you grow up believing you're creative and exciting, changes are good you will be creative and exciting. In all areas of life, we are so much what we think we are. We believe what our mind sees.

We can develop creativity in ourselves simply by seeing ourselves as being creative. So perhaps we should devote less concern to what occurs without and invest more concern toward what is happening within—within ourselves.

ENTREPRENEURIAL CREATIVITY

The term "entrepreneur" is a popular buzz word that is very much intrend as it refers to business. But why can't it apply to our lives? If we think of an entrepreneur as a persion who has a vision and creates something to fill a need in business—whether it be something new or something old which is rearranged—could the concept not be applied to life, also?

Can our lives be thought of as an arena where we can create something new—something we don't have, such as happiness, calmness or professional skills?

If we have trouble filling our own personal needs, perhaps a change is in order. We need the enthusiasm or spirit to challenge who we are and what we want to become. This is no easy challenge. Who we are generally is the product of our perceptions of, and reactions to, our parents, peers, and close friends and culture. It takes real bravery to challenge and change our status quo when our strongest motivation is because we desire a change.

Many people aren't aware of all they can do for themselves. As human beings, we can do things that can positively influence our own attitudes that can help yield desired results. We can create better relationships, wealth, happiness, and full and rewarding lives through personal creativity.

Yet, people often refuse to acknowledge their creative capacities. After so many years of thinking they aren't creative, they become rigid in their thinking. Psychologist Abraham Maslow once said, "People who are only good with hammers see every problem as a nail." For example, suppose the only tool you own is a hammer. If you must nail two boards together, you'll be prepared to do a good job. But what happens when it's time to wash windows and scrub floors? Would you use a hammer for those jobs? Certainly not. So you'll have to find or develop other tools if you want clean windows and floors.

People who operate under strict thought processes and self-imposed limitations are, figuratively speaking, using a hammer to wash windows. Of course, a hammer is an insufficient tool for that job, and the user becomes frustrated. Then, he or she must rely on others to get the job done, live with dirty windows or continue to use the hammer in hopes of some day getting sufficient results.

Naturally, this is not the way to achieve self-reliance, effectiveness and efficiency. Yet, it's the way many people live their lives. They use certain thought processes—or tools, if you will—to solve their problems. When those don't produce positive results, they become frustrated and ineffective.

Taking responsibility for your life does more than just call for creativity. It demands it. Let's take a look at how creative people operate.

(1) **They break routine.** People who follow routine day in and day out often get bored with it, and why not? With an average life span of seventy-plus years, it seems like such a waste for people to spend five to seven days per week, each week of their lives, doing the same thing. Variety is not only the spice of life, but it's also a good way to open your mind to new possibilities. Don't be afraid to do different things. Take a walk during lunch. Find a new route to work. Don't keep your radio dial stuck to the same station. Try something new for dinner. If you like rock music, attend a symphony. If you're a classical music buff, check out a rock concert. Learn to play an instrument. Develop new friendships. Subscribe to a different magazine or newspaper. The world is full of ideas, but you must be exposed to them to get the benefit. After all, consider what might have happened if Ray Kroc had never discovered the McDonald brothers!

(2) **They find alternatives.** You've heard it said that "there's more than one way to skin a cat." The cat-skinner who knows several ways to proceed will be in better shape if the preferred method doesn't work. Doing things a certain way, simply because it's the way it has always been done, really stifles our creativity as unique and wonderful human beings.

(3) **They adapt rather than adopt.** Ray Kroc adapted the McDonald brothers' marketing plan geared for a

relatively small town and made it work from coast-to-coast. That's adaptation, not adoption. Good musicians don't copy other musicians' arrangements; they adapt them to suit their own tastes and styles. Don't be afraid to take other people's ideas and apply them to your own needs. You might develop something unique.

(4) **They ask themselves, "What if?".** Many times, a creative solution can be found simply by setting up imaginary scenarios. Thomas A. Edison probably asked himself "what if?" on a regular basis. For example, he might have asked, "What if a room could be illuminated by electricity?" "What if sounds could be reproduced from a machine?" "What if there were a device that would project pictures in motion on a screen?" In his day, these might have seemed like pretty far-out "what if" questions. But we don't laugh at them anymore because Edison didn't think it silly to seek answers. Don't be afraid to create such imaginary situations. You might create a solution to a problem.

(5) **They do things differently from most people.** Sales trainer Joel Weldon cautions people who would be successful to find out what everyone is doing, then don't do it. The premise is that most people might not be as successful as we'd like to be, so we'd better not act like them.

(6) **They don't impose limitations on themselves.** When the cassette player was introduced, the device was about the size of a suitcase. But because inventors refused to think small, the cassette recorders became smaller and smaller until now, a good system can fit into the palm of your hand. Plug earphones into it, and you have what the Sony company calls a "Walk Man." If inventors had convinced themselves that scaling down

was impossible, cassette recorders probably never would have found their way into people's automobiles—let alone into their shirt pockets.

(7) **They have creative role models and friends.** As we've already seen, when desiring to develop a certain behavior, it's good to have role models and friends who practice that behavior. Likewise, if we want to be creative, it's a good idea to associate with creative people. This is especially true when associating with creative people in our own fields. Ideas can be traded, bounced off each other and reviewed by a panel of creative heads instead of just one.

(8) **They keep life exciting.** Remember that environment of excitement I mentioned in the chapter on attitude? Creative people constantly develop such an environment. Why? Excited people usually are more creative. Excitement is nothing more than the result of stimulation, which can trigger all types of creativity.

(9) **They are focused.** People who are dedicated to an endeavor tend to think in terms of that endeavor during all of their waking hours and, sometimes, even when they sleep. As a result, they frequently look at life in terms of how events can be relevant to their ambitions.

For example, I am so focused on my ambitions as a speaker, seminar leader and consultant that I can't help but automatically be on the lookout for new ideas. When I read something in a newspaper or magazine or see an object, my mind focuses on how I might use it to communicate thoughts on self-improvement. Whether it's a piece of advice or an illustration that makes a point—I determine how I can use it. I once discovered a deflated basketball in my closet and developed an idea from it for a speech to a high school basketball booster organization. The theme of the speech was, "What do players do when the air goes out of the basketball, when the crowds are gone and the games are over?"

Of course, you don't have to be a professional speaker to benefit from creativity. The ability to create answers to questions and solutions to problems is valuable in any profession. And it's vital to help us through personal crises which, in this society, are no strangers to anyone. I'll have more to say about dealing with crises constructively in the next chapter.

CHAPTER HIGHLIGHTS

(1) In business and in life, entrepreneurial creativity isn't so much coming up with new, original thoughts as it is putting old ideas to work in a new way and achieving successful results.

(2) Self-image is the key to all success and failure. Thinking you're not creative is the best way to ensure that you never became creative. In all areas of life, we are what we think we are.

(3) If an entrepreneur is a person who creates something to fill a need in business, then the same concept can be applied to life. As individuals, we can create things we don't have, such as happiness, skills and better relationships, to fill personal needs.

(4) Creative people break routine, find alternatives and adapt others' ideas. They ask themselves "What if?", they do things differently from most people and don't impose limi-

tations on themselves. They have creative role models and friends, they keep life exciting and they are focused.

MY PERSONAL ACTION PLAN

** The most important idea I gained from reading this chapter is: _____

_____ .

** My plan for using this idea is: _____

_____ .

** I will commit to this idea because: _____

_____ .

** The specific actions I will take to implement this idea are: _____

_____

_____ .

** The results I expect from my usage of this idea are: ___

_____

_____ .

Chapter Fifteen

Positive Handling of Crises

Plop-plop, fizz-fizz, oh, what a relief it is! This line, sung to an upbeat tune, sold a lot of Alka-Seltzer tablets in its day. But it also did its part to reinforce the "instant gratification" lifestyle that so many Americans have adopted in recent years.

Virtually everything has become instant in our society. Medicines give us instant relief from pain. Fast food gives us instant relief from hunger. Alcohol, drugs and fast love affairs give us instant relief from emotional discomforts.

The list could go on, but I'm sure you get the picture. As a society, we often seek "quick fixes" for very serious problems, or we look for "band-aid" cures when "major surgery" might be a better solution. When we try to solve our problems by achieving an altered state of consciousness, we generally only mask the problem, rather than eliminate it. When we resume our regular state, our problem remains.

With the exception of the death of an enemy or the winning of a sweepstakes, serious problems won't go away overnight. At least, they never have for me. In the past few years, I've had excellent success in meeting one of my life's biggest challenges—dealing effectively with crises.

Coaching high school basketball was a challenging period in my life. The accumulation of stress kept me in a constant state of physical and emotional turmoil. I would catch a cold or a virus in mid-November, and I wouldn't be able to shake it until March. My hair would gray more, and my facial features would sag. My nose bled frequently, and staying awake at dinner took Herculean effort. If I was seated in a barber's or dentist's chair, I would fall asleep. When I would arise in the morning, I felt as if a truck had hit me. Even though I slept for 12 hours at night, I would still feel very, very tired in the morning. At that time in my life, I just couldn't muster any energy.

But I survived it by changing my habits and attitudes. It took a lot of time and effort. Now, I don't have all the answers, and I'm not sure anyone does. But I've applied what I learned to an acronym that you might find helpful. The acronym is "GAIN TOTAL ENERGY." Let me explain each letter.

G IS FOR "GROWTH"

When we overcome challenges, we grow. Therefore, challenges at least have their good points, because they make us stronger. They give us perspectives in our personal lives to which we can relate.

When someone's heart is shattered by a lost loved one, he or she often is convinced that the best part of life is over. Yet, most of us heal, and we usually find our next relationship to be more successful and rewarding than the one we lost. That's growth. When I lost my coaching job, I thought it was the end of my career. My esteem was shattered. In time, I learned it was only the beginning.

Challenges sometimes are fun. Sometimes, they are horrible. But they always offer us the opportunity to strengthen ourselves. Remember Viktor Frankl in **Man's Search For Meaning.** When faced with a challenge, we can fight it, and the prize is frustration, injury or death. We can resign to it, and the prize is stagnation—a withering away of the spirit. Or we can accept it and deal with it effectively. The prize for that option is growth—the name of the game of life.

Life is a growing process, and growth is a long-term situation. And challenges are the only way we can grow. So learn to accept challenges. In fact, look for them. One thing about a challenge; while learning to deal with it, life seldom is boring.

A IS FOR "AMIABLE AND ABLE"

People with poor self-images chronically devalue themselves. They hold low self-esteem because they've long regarded themselves as inferior people. And because they regard themselves as inferior, others often do, too. And, even if others don't interpret one's behavior as inferior, the person often perceives that they do. And that's enough to cause damage to the self-image, because people who perceive that others don't admire or respect them will devalue themselves even more.

This devaluation leads to a loss of effectiveness and efficiency, because the person who doesn't respect himself or herself generally is incapable of producing good results in an undertaking. Again, it's a self-image problem that only threatens to get worse with time.

If you're afflicted with such a vicious cycle, there is a treatment. By reminding yourself periodically that you are amiable and able, you can lay the groundwork to raise your self-esteem. With a stronger self-image, you'll be better able to cope with life's crises.

It's important for us as individuals to have a strong image of who we are and what we think. Once we have it firmly in mind that we are amiable and able people, there will be no need for apologies, and we can proceed with the business of life—becoming who and what we want to be. And by ridding ourselves of such "psychological trash," we will be able to handle crises with greater confidence and poise.

I IS FOR "INSPIRATIONAL READING"

When you think your climb in life is all uphill, read about the lives of people who really had to struggle, such as Helen Keller, who was born a deaf, blind mute, yet who managed to write more than 25 books; or Abraham Lincoln, who experienced a great deal of personal, professional and political setbacks before becoming the nation's 16th president.

Of course, those aren't the only people who have had hard knocks. Virtually all people who have achieved some fame or greatness in their lives had to pay dearly for it in some way. And it's the price they paid that's inspiring.

The lives of Martin Luther King Jr. and Mahatma Gandhi wouldn't have been as interesting without the struggles and opposition they met trying to free their people. Ludwig von Beethoven wrote symphonies that he never heard because he was deaf—even while he composed them.

In virtually any life, you'll find handicaps, hassles and heartaches. But it seems the successful people are those who aren't willing to be immobilized by these setbacks. Read about these people's lives for inspiration.

N IS FOR "NATURAL HIGH"

Getting high is fun, when it's done naturally. Unfortunately, many people choose to get high artificially, a practice that most often offers unpleasant side-effects. I don't mean to sound like a preacher, but I think there's sufficient documentation to indicate that long-term nicotine, alcohol and drug use can be harmful, if not fatal.

Fortunately, there is no shortage of sources for natural highs. They are common in our everyday environment. The enjoyment of art can produce highs. So can the enjoyment of music—particularly a live concert. Nature can get you high. A sunrise on the east coast or a sunset on the west can flip the "glad-to-be-alive" switch as you walk on the beach. Likewise, a cool mountain breeze can produce the same effect. Treating yourself to a favorite food can also be a sensory experience, along with participating in a favorite sport—especially those that produce real thrills like skiing, skating, parasailing, parachuting or hang-gliding.

To be in optimum condition to handle crises, we must be in optimum condition, period. Keeping our body toxicity to a minimum is essential for good health and resilience.

Perhaps there is no better way to get a natural high than by breathing—deep breathing from the diaphragm, not the chest. When under heavy stress, people tense. We tend to breathe more rapidly than normal. It's part of the body's involuntary response mechanism to situations perceived as threatening. But as a result of consciously taking fewer, but deeper, breaths, the body gets more oxygen and relaxes.

The next time you find yourself suffering from distress, spend a few minutes bringing yourself back to normal by deep breathing. Give it a try. It works.

T IS FOR "TIME MANAGEMENT"

A great deal of our stress and worry results from deadlines that threaten to catch us unprepared. A time crunch can lead to stress, and most time crunches result from poor planning, or no planning at all.

It's amazing how many of life's stresses can be eliminated through proper planning. As we've already seen, determining ambitions, conscientiously maintaining a priority list, a "to-do" list, and a schedule can help you keep track of your time and your commitments. Keeping organized can help you maintain effectiveness and efficiency.

Remember, a large part of how people succeed or fail results from their use of time. The more effectively and efficiently you use it, the better your results will be, the fewer time crunches and hassles you'll create for yourself and, as a result, the better your chances at success.

O IS FOR "OBTAIN HELP"

Sometimes, it's important to know when and where to seek help. Many people perceive asking for help as a sign of personal weakness or failure. Actually, I look at realizing a personal problem and seeking help to correct it as a strength; it's a positive sign that a person truly wants to improve.

Human beings are neither infallible nor invulnerable. The variety of roles we play in life sometimes conflict with each other. We're all subject to personal problems and weaknesses. But it's how we handle those weaknesses that makes or breaks us. Depending on our reaction, we can collapse under pressures, or we can become stronger by overcoming them. Sometimes, the job of overcoming a problem or weakness is too much to be handled alone.

If you're feeling such pressure, don't be afraid to seek help.

T IS FOR "TURN AWAY TOXICS"

The significance of avoiding physical toxics has already been explained, but toxics also come in human and habit form, too.

It's difficult to keep a positive attitude when you're surrounded by people with negative attitudes. Attitudes are contagious—especially negative ones. Of course, we're all responsible for our own attitudes, but keeping negative company is creating a needless challenge.

Also, beware of toxic habits, such as procrastination, goofing off, wasting time and a host of others that won't contribute positively to your life.

And, above all, expel toxic thoughts. People can make you angry only if you let them. When someone acts in a manner that you find offensive or distasteful, you can choose to explode with anger and raise your blood pressure. Or, if that's not your style, you can work on getting an ulcer by stewing in your juices. Or you can simply take note of the person's behavior and then choose to think of other things. Refuse to give the person permission to spoil your day. After all, how long you allow yourself to be miserable is your decision, and yours alone.

A IS FOR ANALYZE

Sometimes, problems aren't the earth-shaking situations we perceive them to be, once we take a good look at them. It's amazing how we can reduce our problems through analyzing them. Discussing problems with our trusted friends often can help us realize solutions that we, alone, might have missed.

Brainstorming with others is a valuable tool for producing positive results. Sometimes, an objective opinion can put the problem in perspective. Other times, having an objective observer might help you discuss the problem rationally. When we're close to a problem, it's difficult to view it rationally, and that's one reason problems often appear greater than they really are.

Sometimes, our problems can be put into perspective by other people's problems. It's like the old saying, "I wept because I had no shoes, until I met someone with no feet." After hearing that my friend, Donna, had committed suicide, I instantly found my personal problems very small by comparison.

It's interesting how quickly our mind focuses on what is truly important in life upon hearing of a friend's misfortune or tragedy. And once we determine what is important, dealing with a problem is merely a matter of acting in our best interests.

L IS FOR "LONG RUN"

Always keep your eye on the big picture. Many times, action to achieve instant relief can cause long-term difficulties. Maintaining control over your life includes looking out for your future, and acting in ways that will generate a higher-caliber of existence for what lies ahead.

By the same token, don't let your vision get so limited that you perceive a disappointing occurrence to be the end of your world. Like with my ill-fated coaching experience, it might be the stepping stone to a new plateau in your career.

E IS FOR ENTHUSIASM

It's easy to get enthusiastic about things we like. But the secret to success is being enthusiastic about things we don't like. Every job is going to have parts that turn us off. But these parts are necessary to the total picture. For example, I know salespeople who love to sell but hate to prospect for new clients. Of course, if they don't prospect, they eventually will run out of clients, and they'll no longer be able to sell. Likewise, I know writers who hate to research. But if they don't research, they'll have nothing to write.

When we look at the big picture to see where these undesirable elements of a job fit in, generating sincere enthusiasm becomes easier. This doesn't mean we have to be all smiles and cheery about having been assigned garbage detail, but it also doesn't mean we have to let it ruin our attitude.

Enthusiasm is an attitude—a zest for life and what we do. And by looking at the big picture, we can create enthusiasm. For example, there are times when I seem to lack the enthusiasm to exercise. But when I look at the benefits it brings—weight control, extra energy, fresh air and sunshine—and the fact that I'll feel physically, mentally and emotionally better after a good run, I become enthusiastic.

Work on creating enthusiasm for things you don't like to do. In time, the enthusiasm will take hold without effort.

N IS FOR NUTRITION

Nutrition is extremely important to one's performance. Yet, many people are deficient in this category. They'll start the day with a sweet roll and coffee with sugar—or, worse yet, a soft drink. Sugar mixed with caffeine might give you a kick to get you going, but it certainly won't give you real energy. It takes more out of the body than it puts in, so it's negative energy at best. At worst, you can find yourself tired and hungry about mid-morning and ready for a nap by mid-afternoon. If this sounds like your situation, try eating some high-protein foods to get you started and keep you going. Meats, cheeses and nuts will suffice if you don't have the time—or the stomach—for sausage and eggs.

Also, if you frequently wake up sluggish, ask yourself when you had your last meal. If it was after 8 o'clock the previous night, your body was using energy to digest your food as you slept. As a result, your sleep might not have been as restful as it could have been.

Maintaining a proper diet is essential for being at your best.

E IS FOR EXERCISE

Exercise serves several purposes. It strengthens our bodies and keeps down our weight, both by burning calories and by decreasing our appetites for food.

Of course, we need food to survive. But perhaps we don't need as much as we think we do. I recall a study dealing with two groups of workers. At mid-day, one group was sent to lunch, and the other was sent for a walk. Not surprisingly, the group that went for the walk had more energy and were more vibrant than the group that had lunch.

When you're feeling tired, perhaps you need something to increase your circulation more than you need something to increase your waistline.

R IS FOR RELAXATION

Of course, we relax while we sleep. But it's very important to me to enjoy periods of conscious relaxation throughout the day.

Just having 15 to 30 minutes to pause and relax is very beneficial to me. It's a perfect time to meditate. And it's the perfect way to recharge while pausing to reflect on whatever is on my mind. This relaxation period is especially helpful if I'm involved in demanding work or am working late into the evening.

G IS FOR GOD

Periods of relaxation also give me a chance to express gratitude or seek guidance through prayer. Believe it or not, it's a real stress-buster. It's also a humbling experience to take troubles to our Maker, who also created the earth, the sun, the planets, the moon and the stars, and to know that He has time for us.

Y IS FOR YOU

You are in charge of your life. Too often, people view their circumstances with remorse, as if they're unable to change them. They resign themselves to their "fate," which often becomes their fate only because they made it so. Certainly, we can't change some circumstances, such as physical handicaps. But we can change many other aspects of our life, provided we're willing to pay the price.

If a situation with which you're unhappy can be changed, change it. If not, make the best of it. Don't spend precious time throwing a "low self-esteem party." We are in charge of our reactions to events and perceptions of our circumstances. And if we're not willing to pay the price for a change, then perhaps it's because the status quo must be more agreeable than we initially thought.

Sometimes, it's difficult to appreciate the positives of a situation when we're so focused on its negatives. By the same token, it always seems the grass is greener on the other side of the fence. As a result, our current situation sometimes seems undesirable and unfulfilling by comparison.

Of course, whether a new situation is an "oasis" or a "mirage" depends totally on you. I cannot, nor can anyone else, determine that for you.

That's why, in the end, it's all up to you. You are in charge.

So, don't drag your way through life. Use the ideas in the acronym to "GAIN TOTAL ENERGY."

CHAPTER HIGHLIGHTS

(1) Growth is the prize for overcoming challenges.

(2) We must remind ourselves that we are amiable and able.

(3) Inspirational reading can help us overcome stress.

(4) Natural highs add enjoyment to life.

(5) Good time-management habits can make us successful.

(6) We can increase our effectiveness by obtaining help when needed.

(7) Turn away toxics of all types to maintain a positive life-style.

(8) Analyze your problems to gain the proper perspective and the best solutions.

(9) Always keep your eye on the big picture to plan your best actions for the long run.

(10) Enthusiasm is essential for outstanding performance.

(11) Good nutrition is required for optimum strength.

(12) Exercise is essential for good health.

(13) Relaxation helps us recharge and recoup from daily demands.

(14) God can help you overcome personal challenges.

(15) You are in charge of your life.

MY PERSONAL ACTION PLAN

****** The most important idea I gained from reading this chapter is: _____

_____.

****** My plan for using this idea is: _____

_____.

****** I will commit to this idea because: _____

_____.

** The specific actions I will take to implement this idea are: _____

_____

_____.

** The results I expect from my usage of this idea are: ___

_____

_____.

Epilogue

Do people work to live, or do they live to work?

Regardless of how you answer that question, you undoubtedly understand that most of us spend a major part of our lives in our careers. And since most of us very much depend on our incomes for survival and for the enjoyment of life, I'd say it was evident that most of us work to live.

But I'm sure you know of people who don't fit into that category. You might even be one yourself. Although they've already achieved financial independence, they don't retire. They continue to work because they enjoy their careers and would prefer death to retirement. These people no longer have to work to live. They live to work.

So why can't you do both? Even if you must work to live, why can't you also live to work? It isn't necessary to be financially independent to enjoy your career. If we look at our lives as creative entrepreneurial experiences, and we realize that a major portion of our lives are spent in our careers, then shouldn't this time be enjoyable?

If we had nine lives like the proverbial cat, it might not be so important that we enjoy our careers this time around. After all, we'd have eight more chances to get it right. But life is a one-shot deal. If you spend it doing something you don't enjoy, you've wasted it. To me, that's a sin, and it's one I don't want to confess to my maker.

Your career doesn't have to be the most important part of your life. But if you want a good life, it had better at least rank among the top five.

THE CHANGING CAREER

It's vital that we understand that careers are ever changing. To be truly effective as entrepreneurs, we must always be ready to go on to the next experience. Preparing for the next job is not something we do every five to 10 years or so. Instead, it's a way of life. I try to live my life in preparation for the next job. I'm constantly educating myself, making myself aware of my capabilities and my potential for growth. This way, I'm in the best position to be prepared for the next job, whenever it develops.

If you're doing the same thing, great! If not, I'd like to challenge you to do so. To my way of thinking, careers were meant to be enjoyed. When we roll out of bed and put our feet on the floor, we should be excited and enthusiastic about going to work. If we find ourselves dreading our jobs, then we're either in the wrong careers or working at the wrong places.

Life was meant to be enjoyed. If we can't find a job that satisfies us, perhaps we can create our own jobs out of our own interests. Entrepreneurs do this every day. They create lucrative situations for themselves by doing what they enjoy. After a brief but successful career as a school teacher, I realized that I really enjoyed teaching, entertaining and communicating. But I also realized that history—though one of my favorite subjects—was not what I wanted to teach.

I had always had a preoccupation with human achievement, excellence and performance, and I wanted to teach on those topics. And I did teach about it during my "Success With Mess" classes, which the school system allowed me to teach for six weeks of the year. But six weeks wasn't enough. I wanted to teach "success" full-time. And what better place is there to teach about human achievement than from the podium as a professional speaker?

THE BENEFITS OF CAREER ENJOYMENT

If more people built careers around things they enjoyed, think of the results! People would be happier with the way they spent a major portion of their lives. Self-images would soar, and personal productivity would increase. People would feel better about themselves and their situations. As a result, they'd take better care of themselves, live longer and be happier and more fulfilled. There would be fewer alcoholics, drug addicts and criminals, not to mention people with anxiety attacks, ulcers and nervous breakdowns.

But let's not limit our sights to just the individual. Think of the benefits to the nation as a whole if people would devote their lives to careers they enjoyed. If people would be more productive at careers they liked, they would turn out better products and services. As a result, the American consumer would reap the benefits. And when the American consumer benefits, the nation's economy gets stronger.

As I see it, the American economy could use the boost that a nation of satisfied consumers could give it. I think part of the problem with the economy is that American consumers are dissatisfied with what is happening in the country. The quality of products and services—not to mention customer service in general—has sunk below an acceptable level. As a result, consumers have sought out goods and services from abroad to obtain better quality.

For so long, America was accustomed to being at the "top of the heap." But with intense foreign competition, America's production has fallen. The poor quality of American products and services is almost regarded as a symptom of the illness that plagues the country, not only in a business sense, but in a personal sense as well. People feel that they have no control over their lives. In response, they take little or no pride in their production.

This does not have to be a permanent standard. If individuals in this country would take responsibility for their own happiness and fulfillment, collectively we could raise the living standard to unprecedented heights. We could regain the confidence of American consumers, and restore America to its place at the top.

And that's why I wrote this book. If your life situation isn't satisfactory, I hope you'll take every measure to change it for the better. It's your life, and no one else will or can change it for you.

The sooner we get started, the sooner we'll see results. Good luck, and Godspeed on your voyage to become the best you are!

MY PERSONAL ACTION PLAN

** The most important idea I gained from reading this book is: _____

_____ .

** My plan for using this idea is: _____

_____ .

** I will commit to this idea because: _____

_____ .

** The specific actions I will take to implement this idea
are: _____

_____

_____ .

** The results I expect from my usage of this idea are: ___

_____

_____ .

For Further Information

For information on Jack's availability to speak at your next meeting, or for questions regarding this book and other Jack Messenger products, write Mr. Jack Messenger, 2108 Cedar Run, #101, Camp Hill, Pennsylvania 17011 or call (717)975-0644.